Scrapbooking Childhood Moments

200 Page Designs

Scrapbooking Childhood Moments

200 Page Designs

Karen Delquadro

Sterling Publishing Co., Inc.
New York
A Sterling / Chapelle Book

Chapelle, Ltd:

Jo Packham, Sara Toliver, Cindy Stoeckl

Cathy Sexton, Editor

Caroll Shreeve, Editorial Director

Karla Haberstich, Art Director

Kim Taylor, Graphic Illustrator

Marilyn Goff, Copy Editor

Staff: Burgundy Alleman, Areta Bingham, Ray Cornia, Emily K. Frandsen, Susan Jorgensen, Barbara Milburn, Lecia Monsen, Karmen Quinney, Desirée Wybrow

Photography: Kevin Dilley for Hazen Imaging, Inc.

Library of Congress Cataloging-in-Publication Data Available

If you have any questions or comments or would like information on specialty products featured in this book, please contact:
Chapelle, Ltd., Inc.
P.O. Box 9252
Ogden, UT 84409
(801) 621-2777 • (801) 621-2788 Fax
e-mail: chapelle@chapelleltd.com
web site: www.chapelleltd.com

The written instructions, projects, and photographs in this volume are intended for the personal use of the reader. Any other use, especially commercial use, is forbidden under law without the written permission of the copyright holder.

This volume is meant to stimulate decorating ideas. If readers are unfamiliar or not proficient in a skill necessary to attempt a project, we urge that they refer to an instructional book specifically addressing the technique required.

Every effort has been made to ensure that all the information in this book is accurate. However, due to differing conditions, tools, and individual skills, the publisher cannot be responsible for any injuries, losses, and/or other damages which may result from the use of the information in this book.

10 9 8 7 6 5 4 3 2 1

Published by Sterling Publishing Co., Inc.
387 Park Avenue South, New York, NY 10016
© 2003 by Karen Delquadro
Distributed in Canada by Sterling Publishing
c/o Canadian Manda Group, One Atlantic Avenue, Suite 105
Toronto, Ontario, Canada M6K 3E7
Distributed in Great Britain by Chrysalis Books
64 Brewery Road, London N7 9NT, England
Distributed in Australia by Capricorn Link (Australia) Pty. Ltd.
P.O. Box 704, Windsor, NSW 2756, Australia
Printed in China

Sterling ISBN 1-4027-0678-2

To Hollee for inspiring me.
To Connie for encouraging me.
To Mom for believing in me.
To Olivia—the love of my life!

You're nobunny til somebunny loves You!

Contents

Preface 8

General Information 8

Chapter 1: Making Memories 10

Chapter 2: Sharing Special Times 40

Chapter 3: Family Fun 64

Chapter 4: Candid Moments 86

A Note from the Author 126

Metric Conversion Chart 126

Index 127

Preface

Welcome to my world of scrapbooking ideas and page designs.

This book was written on the premise that you already know the basics of scrapbooking—from knowing how to use the basic tools to being familiar with simple techniques such as photo matting.

As you have probably already figured out, scrapbooking is a very personal form of art and can be presented on many different levels. Some scrapbookers want their scrapbooks to be absolutely precise with all of their pictures perfectly aligned on the page, photo mats cut with exact precision, and journaling to be done to perfection. Other scrapbookers enjoy a more relaxed look and feel to their pages—using torn-paper photo mats and page borders, natural fibers such as raffia and jute, and all of the cutting and placement done simply without a lot of fuss.

The scrapbook page designs presented here were created with a primitive flair. Many of the pages were created with natural earthtone shades to enhance my love of nature and for natural things—including the love I have for all of my scrapbook subjects!

—Karen Delquadro

General Information

The pages presented in this volume were created in a double-page format on both 8 1/2" x 11" and 12" x 12" pages. Each spread includes a complete supply list for creating the featured pages, in addition to offering general how-to instructions on a special technique used on that spread.

The first time a particular method is presented, the instructions are included. The concept for each page design then builds on that idea, offering a new idea with each subsequent scrapbook page. If you see something on a page that is not explained, simply refer back to previous pages or the index.

Because the pages presented here have been created with many fun dimensional objects, such as beads, buttons, brads, and ribbons, the archival-quality of the scrapbook pages has been compromised. You will also want to use page protectors that have been specifically designed for this type of scrapbooking and store these albums upright. We very much encourage you to keep your treasured archival volumes separate from your fun, day-to-day dimensional albums.

Choosing an Adhesive

There are several archival-quality adhesives on the market that work great for scrapbooks. The trick is finding the one best suited to you and your style of scrapbooking.

When adhering photographs to cardstock for matting purposes, double-sided adhesive tabs are widely used. Glue sticks also work well and are inexpensive. They are however messier to use.

When attaching dimensional objects, such as buttons, scrapbook glue is recommended. This type of adhesive is a heavy-duty glue manufactured specifically for this purpose.

Journaling

Journaling on your pages is probably the most important element when scrapbooking.

Some scrapbookers are hesitant to do much journaling because they either don't like their handwriting or they aren't quite confident enough to know what to write or how to write it. Don't let these fears deter you—there is nothing more special than personalizing something in one's own handwriting and dialect. This gives added enjoyment when the scrapbooks are passed down from generation to generation.

Handwritten vs Computer-generated Journaling

There are pros and cons to both methods of journaling, but handwritten journaling adds the finishing touches to the personalization of the project. Many scrapbookers would prefer to use a computer for their journaling because they don't believe their handwriting is nice enough. Other scrapbookers wouldn't dream of using anything but their own penmanship on their pages—another confirmation that scrapbooking is a unique art form based strictly on the individual taste of the scrapbook artist.

Most of the pages in this volume have been hand-lettered. On the pages that have been computer-generated, the sentiments were typed and then printed directly on a full sheet of cardstock. It is impossible to put scraps of cardstock

through your printer. In addition, keep in mind that many printers cannot accommodate the thickness of a sheet of cardstock, so hand-lettering may be your only option. One alternative is to print your sentiments out on bond paper—white or colored—then adhere it to cardstock.

An important point to consider when choosing between handwriting and computer-generated journaling is which of the methods is archival. Unless you have the luxury of printing from a laser printer, the best choice would be handwriting. Ink-jet printers are not archival quality and over time the ink will fade and can actually chip off the page. Handwriting done with archival journaling markers is timeless.

8½" x 11" Pages vs 12" x 12" Pages

The size of the pages you choose is purely personal preference. There are advantages to using both sizes.

The products in both sizes are readily available and the selection is enormous. Scrapbooking has taken the world by storm and most craft-type stores have huge sections dedicated to scrapbook supplies and support products.

A Special Girl

Supplies

Background Cardstock:
Stonewashed Blue, Stonewashed Green

Layout Cardstock:
Recycled Brick Red

Vellum: Clear

Paper Punch:
Daisy

Silk Ribbon, $1/4$" Wide: Red

Adhesive

Journaling Markers:
Assorted Colors

Two-toned Horizontal Backgrounds

- Beginning along the top edge of a single sheet of cardstock, cut it horizontally to the desired height. Beginning along the bottom edge of the same sheet of cardstock, cut it horizontally to the desired height.

- Position the cardstock strips, aligning them along one horizontal side of each sheet of background cardstock. In this case, one strip was positioned along the bottom of one sheet of background cardstock and the remaining strip was positioned along the top of the remaining sheet of background cardstock.

Layered Paper-punch Embellishment

- Punch daisies from the cardstock and the vellum.

- Layer and adhere each cardstock daisy on top of each vellum daisy. Draw the center of each daisy.

Helping Hands

Supplies

Background Cardstock:
Navy Blue, Stonewashed Green

Layout Cardstock:
Goldenrod

Rubber Stamp:
Handprints

Stamp Pad:
Black

Adhesive

Journaling Markers:
Assorted Colors

Torn-paper Page Borders

- Beginning along the left edge of a single sheet of cardstock, tear it vertically in an uneven manner to the desired width. Beginning along the right edge of the same sheet of cardstock, tear it vertically similar to the previous strip. Repeat with a second sheet of cardstock so you have four vertical cardstock strips.

- Position the cardstock strips, aligning them along each vertical side of each sheet of background cardstock.

FYI: If desired, a single sheet of cardstock can be torn vertically twice so you have a vertical strip of cardstock with both vertical edges torn. This cardstock strip can be adhered to the center of a single sheet of cardstock to achieve the same effect.

Red Rock Ruins

Supplies

Background Cardstock:
Recycled Buckskin

Layout Cardstock:
Dark Brown

Patterned Paper:
Kokopelli & Spiral Suns

Paper Punches:
Gecko, Large Spiral,
Small Spiral, Small Triangle

Adhesive

Journaling Marker:
Black

Layered Torn-paper Page Borders & Torn-paper Photo Mats

- Beginning along the left edge of a single sheet of cardstock, tear it vertically in an uneven manner to the desired width. Beginning along the right edge of the same sheet of cardstock, tear it vertically similar to the previous strip.

- Repeat with the patterned paper, making two vertical strips. These strips should be slightly narrower than the cardstock strips.

- Position the cardstock strips, aligning them along opposite vertical sides of each sheet of background cardstock. Layer the patterned paper strips on top of the cardstock strips, aligning them along the same vertical sides.

- Adhere each photograph onto an appropriately sized piece of cardstock. Carefully tear the cardstock around the photograph to create a unique photo mat.

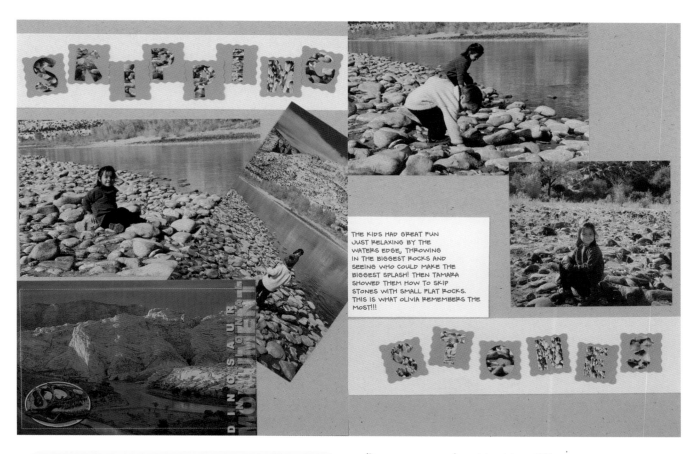

THE KIDS HAD GREAT FUN
JUST RELAXING BY THE
WATERS EDGE, THROWING
IN THE BIGGEST ROCKS AND
SEEING WHO COULD MAKE THE
BIGGEST SPLASH! THEN TAMARA
SHOWED THEM HOW TO SKIP
STONES WITH SMALL FLAT ROCKS.
THIS IS WHAT OLIVIA REMEMBERS THE
MOST!!!

Skipping Stones

Supplies

Background Cardstock:
Recycled Tan

Layout Cardstock:
Moss Green,
Recycled Ivory, White

Paper Punches:
Alphabet, Scalloped Blocks

Adhesive

Journaling Marker:
Black

Paper-punched Letter Tiles

- Punch several blocks from the cardstock.

- Punch the necessary letters for the sentiment you have chosen from portions of photographs that have been cropped away or from your duplicate photographs. In this case, the letters were punched from photographs of the stones around the lake.

- Layer the letters on top of the cardstock blocks, centering each letter inside each block.

- Randomly position the letter tiles on horizontal strips of cardstock.

FYI: When making letter tiles, try hand-lettering or using letter stickers and/or rubber-stamped letters. The "tiles" can also be cut from cardstock instead of punched. Keep in mind that various-sized tiles add interest when used on the same scrapbook page. To add dimension, place a foam dot under each letter tile.

SeXToN FAMILY

Formal Family Photos

Supplies

Background Cardstock: Chocolate

Layout Cardstock: Black, Brown, Light Tan

Patterned Papers: Leopard Print Assortment

Photo Corners: Black • Paper Punches: Alphabet

Fibers • Adhesive • Journaling Marker: Black

Matching Patterned Papers to Wardrobe Fabrics

- Look for patterned papers that will coordinate with or match the wardrobe fabrics shown in your photographs.

In this case, a variety of leopard-print papers was used to highlight the "wild" side of this family's garments.

- Randomly tear each patterned paper into photo mats and/or page borders.

- Layer, alternating with torn-edged cardstock, as desired and adhere in place.

For Mother's Day we spent the morning at the park. I will never forget the beautiful day we shared. I watched you study the log, and look at it with intense curiosity. Moments like these, fill me with the awe of your individuality. I love you so much, that it is hard to believe that we are actually different people, but I will always make sure you grow into the person you are capable of being, by letting you be the individual person that God intended you to be.

Mom...

Mother's Day

Supplies

Background Cardstock: Spice

Layout Cardstock:
Forest Green, Spice

Vellum: Clear

Patterned Vellum:
Muted Floral with Leaves

Silk Ribbon, $1^1/_2$" Wide:
Moss Green

Adhesive

Journaling Marker: Black

Silk-ribbon Embellishment

- Tie an appropriately sized bow from the silk ribbon and position it so it will enhance your photograph.

- Cut a length from the silk ribbon and wrap it around the corner of a photograph or box of journaling.

- Cut each exposed ribbon tail at an angle to help prevent it from fraying.

Layered Photo Mats

- Adhere each photograph onto an appropriately sized piece of cardstock. Carefully cut the cardstock around the photograph, keeping the same border width around all sides.

- Add one or more additional pieces of coordinating or contrasting cardstock. Mat widths can be uniform or can vary with each layer.

A Summer Day

Supplies

Background Cardstock: Recycled Kraft

Layout Cardstock:
Soft Moss Green, Recycled Ivory

Silk Ribbon, $1^1/_2$" Wide: Metallic Red

Stickers: Pressed Flowers

Hole Punch: $^1/_8$" Diameter

Craft Wire: 24-gauge Silver-toned

Round Toothpick

Adhesive

Journaling Marker: Black

Craft Wire Embellishment

- Punch holes into the cardstock as desired to accommodate each end of the length of wire.

- To create the "pig tails," rap the length of wire around a toothpick. Remove the wire from the toothpick and adjust the "curls" as desired.

- Thread the curled wire through the punched holes in the cardstock.

- Lengths of straight wire can also be twisted together to replicate chicken wire. If necessary, wire can be threaded through holes that have been punched in the background cardstock to help stabilize long lengths of wire embellishment.

FYI: Craft wire is available in many different colors and in several sizes. Keep in mind that the smaller the gauge size number the bigger around the wire will be.

Pumpkin Patch

Supplies

Background Cardstock: Olive Green, Yellow Green

Layout Cardstock: Olive Green, Mustard • Vellum: Clear

Stickers: Harvest Assortment, Letters & Numbers

Miniature Brads: Gold-toned • String: Brown

Adhesive • Journaling Marker: Black

Mixing Black-and-White & Color Photographs

- Take several shots with colored film, then take several more with black-and-white film. The combination, used together on the same scrapbook page or spread, adds unusual dimension.

Miniature Brad Embellishment

- Push the post at the back of each miniature brad through the cardstock and/or photograph, then flatten out each side of the post at the back side to secure.

- Embroidery floss, jute, raffia, string, or thread can be wrapped around each brad to make the item attached by the brads appear to be hanging. The ends can be tucked behind the cardstock or left to hang at random.

Family ties

We love to pack up our families and get back to nature!

Family Ties

Supplies

Background Cardstock: Brick Red, Recycled Buckskin

Layout Cardstock: Navy Blue, Dark Brown, Burgundy, Rust, Tan

Vellum: Clear • Miniature Brads: Black

Jute: Natural • Raffia: Natural • Strings: Brown, Burgundy

Hole Punch: $^1/_8$" Diameter

Adhesive • Journaling Markers: Assorted Colors

Hand-cut Tags

- Cut tags from various colors of cardstock. Cut the tags straight across the top or with angled corners.

- Layering the tags with different colors of cardstock adds dimension.

- To combine layered tags, punch holes into the cardstock as desired to accommodate each end of the length of jute, raffia, or string.

- Thread the fiber through the punched holes. Tie the fiber ends into a knot to secure.

- Attach the tags to your scrapbook page(s) with adhesive or miniature brads.

- Write an appropriate sentiment for the theme of your scrapbook page(s) on each tag.

Easter Favorites

Supplies

Background Cardstock: Pastel Green • Layout Cardstock: Assorted Colors

Die-cut Tag: Yellow • Metal-rimmed Tags, Assorted Shapes: Blue, Yellow

Raffia: Lavender, Natural, Teal • Strings: Black, White, Yellow

Paper Punches: Bunny, Carrot, Duck, Egg • Hole Punch: $1/8$" Diameter

Craft Wires: 26-gauge Black, 24-gauge Brown

Adhesive • Journaling Markers: Assorted Colors

Die-cut & Metal-rimmed Tags

- Embellish each tag with shapes punched from cardstock. Overlap the punched shapes to add interest.

- If desired, write a word or phrase on each tag.

- If desired, draw a decorative border around the outside perimeter of one or more of the tags you are using.

- Attach the tags to your scrapbook page(s) with adhesive or miniature brads.

FYI: Die-cut and metal-trimmed tags are available in an assortment of colors and have a single hole in each tag for hanging.

Jute, raffia, or string can be threaded through the holes and tied as desired.

Thank Heaven for Little Girls

Supplies

Background Cardstock: Hot Pink

Layout Cardstock: Hot Pink

Vellum: Clear • Patterned Vellum: Pink Plaid

Paper Punch: Flower

Metal-rimmed Tag, Circle: Pink

Hole Punch: $1/8$" Diameter

Eyelets: Purple, White, Yellow

Adhesive • Journaling Marker: Black

Eyelets In a Functional Capacity

- Determine what you are going to attach to your scrapbook page(s) with eyelets. In this case, the flowers and the *metal-rimmed tag*.

- Determine the placement of the eyelet. In this case, the eyelets were placed at the centers of the flowers and through the preexisting hole in the *metal-rimmed tag*.

- Punch a hole through each flower and through the paper and/or cardstock in which they are to be attached.

- Place one eyelet through the hole in each flower and position them over the holes in the background paper and/or cardstock. Using an eyelet setter and a hammer, permanently set the eyelet into position. Make certain you do this procedure on a cutting mat or board.

Girl Power

Supplies

Background Cardstock:
Lavender, Light Pink

Layout Cardstock:
Assorted Colors

Stickers: Flowers, Letters

Metal-rimmed Tags, Assorted Shapes:
Lavender, Lime Green, Hot Pink

Hole Punch: $1/8$" Diameter

Eyelets: Green, Pink, Purple

Adhesive

Journaling Marker: Black

Eyelets In a Decorative Capacity

- Generally eyelets are used as a method for attaching items to your scrapbook page(s). However, eyelets can be used as a design element. Place eyelets decoratively as desired. In this case, three purple eyelets are in a horizontal row.

- Punch a series of holes through the background cardstock.

- Place one eyelet through each hole. Using an eyelet setter and a hammer, permanently set the eyelet into position. Make certain you do this procedure on a cutting mat or board.

FYI: Miniature brads can be substituted for eyelets to add a similar decorative element to your scrapbook page(s).

Everything Tastes Better at Grandma's

Supplies

Background Cardstock: Recycled Off-white

Layout Cardstock: Black, Dark Brown, Christmas Red, Dark Red, White

Hole Punch: 1/4" Diameter

Eyelet: White • Miniature Brad: Black

Strings: Dark Brown, White • Adhesive

Journaling Markers: Assorted Colors

String Art

- Position the white string in a free-form design to replicate a cooked spaghetti noodle. Secure in position with scrapbook glue.

- Tear "meatballs" from cardstock and glue in place as desired.

Single Photo-corner Accent

- Cut a square from the cardstock to the desired dimensions.

- Tear the square into a triangle, leaving two of the sides straight.

- Adhere the triangle in place on one of the corners of your photograph.

- Accent the single photo corner with a single eyelet in a contrasting color to the cardstock.

TO MY LITTLE LOVE BUG, you say you love me more than all the houses, all the cars, all the trees and all the stars, stacked up on top of each other... well, I love you that much...times a million gillion....

Mom

A Special Boy

Supplies

Background Cardstock: Recycled White

Layout Cardstock:
Dark Red, Recycled White

Photo Corners: Black

Patterned Vellum: Embossed Hearts

Hole Punch: ⅛" Diameter

Eyelets: Red • Embroidery Floss: Black

Buttons: Black, White

Adhesive

Journaling Marker: Black

Lacing Eyelets

- Set a series of eyelets into position as desired.
- Using a needle threaded with embroidery floss, begin lacing the eyelets. Continue until each eyelet has been sewn through three or four times. Tie the floss ends into a knot to secure.

Glued-button Embellishment

- Position the buttons in small clusters as desired. Secure them in place with scrapbook glue.

Falling in Love with the Ocean

Supplies

Background Cardstock: Goldenrod

Layout Cardstock: Steel Blue • Glass Bead: Clear

Hole Punch: $1/8$" Diameter

Jute: Black, Natural

Charms: Brass Hearts, Pewter Sand Dollar

Memorabilia Pocket • Seashells

Adhesive

Journaling Markers: Assorted Colors

Glass Bead Embellishment

- Write an appropriate sentiment for the theme of your scrapbook page(s). The word you want to "highlight" should be written small enough so the entire word fits underneath the glass bead.

- Adhere the glass bead centered over the word. The word will appear to be somewhat magnified.

Charm Embellishment

- Thread jute through the holes in the tops of the charms, then tie into a knot to secure.

- Thread the charms onto a length of jute in a clothesline manner, then secure both ends of the jute at the back side of the cardstock.

Memorabilia Pocket Embellishment

- Place desired items inside memorabilia pockets, then adhere in place on your scrapbook page(s).

Silly Friends

Supplies

Background Cardstock: Sky Blue, Steel Blue

Layout Cardstock:
Light Blue, Navy Blue, Olive Green, White

Vellum: Clear • Iron-on: Beach Sandals

Die-cut Tags: White

Metal-rimmed Tag, Circle: Yellow

String: White • Embroidery Floss: Blue

Paper Punch: Fish • Hole Punch: $^1/_8$" Diameter

Raffia: Natural • Rhinestones • Pearl • Starfish

Mesh • Terry Cloth • Adhesive

Journaling Markers: Assorted Colors

Rhinestone Embellishment

• Position rhinestones in small clusters as desired. Secure them in place with scrapbook glue.

Torn-paper Art

• Tear a scrap of cardstock into the shape desired. In this case, a fish.

Vellum-wrapped & Stitched Cardstock

• Tear a scrap of vellum into a square or rectangle along all four sides.

• Place a piece of cardstock on top of the torn piece of vellum. Wrap the vellum over the top and bottom of the cardstock. Crease along the top and bottom edges.

• Punch a series of holes along the top and bottom edges of the vellum. Stitch together with embroidery floss in a random manner to encase the cardstock. Tie the floss ends into a knot to secure.

family
Sledding
day

Family Sledding Day

Supplies
Background Cardstock: Olive Green

Layout Cardstock: Metallic Gold, Ivory, Kraft, Purple, Recycled White, Yellow

Photo Corners: Kraft Paper • String: Natural

Memorabilia Pocket • Paper Punch: Snowflake

Hole Punch: $1/8$" Diameter • Eyelets: Purple

Adhesive • Journaling Marker: Black

Multicolored Photo Mats

- Cut a mat from one color of cardstock for each of your photographs.

- Cut or tear strips from multi-colored cardstock scraps and layer on top of each mat.

- Trim the excess so the scraps are flush with the outside edges of the mats.

FYI: You will want each mat to have an entirely different look. This helps add interest and dimension to your scrapbook page(s).

Wound-string Embellishment

- Randomly wind string around a matted photograph or sentiment box.

- Tie the string ends into a knot to secure.

Huntin' Wabbits

Supplies

Background Cardstock: Brown

Layout Cardstock: Dark Brown, Olive Green

Patterned Paper: Brown & Green Plaid

Hole Punch: $1/8$" Diameter • Embroidery Floss: Black

Miniature Brads: Copper

Meshes: Black, Green

Metal Tags:
Rectangle, Circle with Engraved Letter

Craft Wire: 24-gauge Copper

Adhesive

Journaling Markers: Assorted Colors

Mesh Embellishment

- Cut a piece of mesh to the desired shape and size. Fray the ends as desired.

- Secure the mesh in place with scrapbook glue.

Hanging Signs

- Push the post at the back of each miniature brad through the background cardstock, then flatten out each side of the post at the back side of the background cardstock to secure.

- Punch one hole into each top corner of the signs you want to hang. Thread embroidery floss through the holes and tie the floss ends into a knot to secure.

- Wrap the floss loop on each sign around one brad to make the signs appear to be hanging.

Ahoy Matey

Supplies

Background Cardstock: Brown

Layout Cardstock:
Black, Dark Green, Olive Green, Ivory

Patterned Paper: Barnwood

Mesh: Green • Jute: Natural

Stickers: Letters

Paper Ribbon: Ivory

Photo Overlay: Olive Green

Plastic Charm: Ship Wheel

Adhesive

Journaling Marker: Black

Photo Overlays

- Remove the precut squares from the photo overlay and clean up any cardstock "burrs" along the edges.

- Save the precut squares to use for letter tiling on these scrapbook pages or for use in the future.

- Adhere the photo overlay over a photograph.

Letter Sticker Tiles

- Place one letter sticker on top of each cardstock square, centering each letter inside each square. In this case, the precut squares that were removed from the photo overlay were used.

- Add a second layer of cardstock behind each letter tile.

- Randomly position the letter tiles on your scrapbook page(s).

FALL of 201

Fall Leaves

Supplies

Background Cardstock: Cinnamon, Olive Green

Layout Cardstock: Cream, Olive Green, Ivory, Mustard

Precut Tags: Kraft Paper

Jute: Natural • String: Natural • Meshes: Black, Brown

Stickers: Letters & Numbers • Hole Punch: $1/8$" Diameter

Adhesive • Journaling Marker: Black

Torn Tags

- Embellish each tag with a contrasting color of cardstock and letter and/or number stickers.

- Tear the bottom of each tag to the desired size.

- Adhere the tags to the scrapbook page(s). To make it look as though the tags are sewn onto your scrapbook page, sew through the holes in the tags with jute, then tie the jute ends into a knot to secure.

Hand-sewn Embellishment

- Punch holes through the background cardstock and photo mats as desired to accommodate your stitching.

- Using a needle threaded with string, begin sewing through the holes. Tie the string ends into a knot in the front or in the back to secure.

Avery
a.k.a.
"boy
wonder"

Boy Wonder

Supplies
Background Cardstock: Olive Green

Layout Cardstock: Olive Green, Periwinkle

Handmade Paper: White • Raffia: Natural

Embroidery Floss: Black

Miniature Brads: Black

Adhesive • Journaling Marker: Black

listen
to the
world
at play

Torn Handmade Paper

- Randomly tear a piece from the handmade paper. In this case, tear the dandelion.

- Position the piece as desired and secure it in place. In this case, additional small pieces were added as "seeds."

FYI: If the handmade paper is difficult to tear, lightly mist it with a spray bottle of water. Once it is slightly damp, tearing it should be a little easier to tear into the desired shape.

Make certain the handmade paper is completely dry before continuing with its use.

Wound Embroidery Floss Embellishment

- Randomly wind embroidery floss around a matted photograph or sentiment box.

- Tie the floss ends into a knot to secure.

Beach Bums

Supplies

Background Cardstock:
Olive Green, Khaki

Layout Cardstock:
Navy Blue, Light Green, Pink, Yellow

Handmade Paper:
White

Vellum: Clear

Miniature Brads: Gold-toned

Adhesive

Journaling Marker: Black

Tea-dyed Handmade Paper

• Lightly mist the areas of the handmade paper you desire to be stained with a spray bottle of diluted tea. Make certain the handmade paper is completely dry before continuing with its use.

Vertical Strips with *Vellum* Overlays

• Cut several narrow strips in varying lengths from the colored cardstock and/or handmade paper.

• Position each series of cardstock strips in a vertical format spaced approximately $1/8$" apart.

• Randomly tear the vellum into squares. One square will be needed for each series of colored cardstock strips.

• Attach each piece of vellum over the series of colored cardstock strips with one miniature brad positioned at each corner.

Sugar & Spice

Supplies

Background Cardstock: Olive Green

Layout Cardstock:
Navy Blue, Lavender, Purple

Die-cut Tag: White

Assorted Beads: Shades of Pink

Embroidery Floss: Pink

Hole Punch: $1/8$" Diameter

Jute: Navy Blue

Adhesive

Journaling Markers: Assorted Colors

Threaded-bead Embellishment

- Punch one hole at each side of a cardstock strip.

- Thread an assortment of beads onto a length of embroidery floss. Thread each floss end through one of the holes and tie the floss ends into a knot to secure.

Bead Dangle Embellishment

- Determine the length of the bead dangle. Allow plenty of extra embroidery floss for wrapping around photo mats.

- Tie a knot at one end of the length of floss.

- Thread an assortment of beads onto the floss so the first bead rests on the knot.

- Tie a knot just after the last bead to keep the beads snugly together.

- Wrap the excess floss around a single photo mat as desired.

Precious One

Supplies

Background Cardstock:
Gray

Handmade Paper:
White

Microbeads:
Silver

Adhesive

Journaling Marker:
Black

Microbead Embellishment

- Place an adequate amount of scrapbook glue in the shape(s) desired on your scrapbook page(s).

- Sprinkle a generous amount of microbeads over the glue. Let dry and tap the background cardstock on your working surface to remove excess microbeads. Return them to their container for later use.

FYI: Microbeads can be found in craft-type stores and are available in a myriad of wonderful colors. They are best adhered with scrapbook glue, but can be affixed with double-sided adhesive tabs.

Stop & Smell the Roses

Supplies

Background Cardstock: Gray

Layout Cardstock: Light Peach

Jute: Dark Green

Decorative Scissors: Scallop-edged

Hole Punch: $1/16$" Diameter

Clusters of Miniature Silk Roses on Stems

Adhesive

Journaling Marker: Black

Hole-punched Cardstock Lace

- Trim the outer edges of the cardstock photo mats and all additional decorative cardstock strips with the scallop-edged decorative scissors.

- To make the cardstock lace, punch one hole in each of the individual scallops on the decorative cardstock strips.

Hand-folded Envelope for Silk Roses

- Starting with a square of cardstock, fold the edges in from both sides, one over the other. Secure on the back side.

Angels in the Garden

Supplies

Background Cardstock: Dark Brown

Layout Cardstock: Goldenrod, Olive Green, Mustard, Rust, White

Cardstock Scraps: Assorted Colors • Vellum: Green

Handmade Paper: Green, White • Raffia: Natural

Paper Punches: Feet, Tiny Flowers, Star • Embroidery Floss: White

Adhesive • Journaling Markers: Assorted Colors

Handmade-paper Art

- Randomly tear each color of handmade paper into pieces of the desired shapes.

- Beginning with the bottom layer, position the pieces and secure them in place. In this case, the cloud was adhered to the background card-stock. The torn-vellum wings were next, followed by the angel's body. The face and feet were added by carefully lifting up a tiny section of the body and inserting them underneath.

- Additional embellishment, such as the hair and the halo, can be added last.

Sisters by Chance
Friends by Choice

Supplies

Background Cardstock: Navy Blue

Layout Cardstock:
Brown, Rust, Tan

Hole Punch: 1/8" Diameter

Eyelets: Blue

Craft Wire:
24-gauge Copper

Adhesive

Journaling Marker: Black

Hanging Looped-wire Embellishment

- Cut and/or tear two similar-sized squares from coordinating colors of cardstock.

- Set one eyelet centered at the top of each double-layered cardstock square.

- Thread a short length of wire through each eyelet and twist the ends together.

- To add several squares together in a clothesline manner, set one eyelet at each side of the background cardstock. Starting and ending at the back side of the cardstock, thread wire through one eyelet, through each of the wire loops on the cardstock squares, then through the remaining eyelet. Twist the wire ends at the back side of the background cardstock to secure.

Wyatt

MAMMA'S, DON'T ♪ LET YOUR BABIES GROW UP TO BE COWBOYS, DON'T LET 'EM PICK ♪ GUITARS AND DRIVE THEM OLD TRUCKS, LET 'EM BE DOCTORS AND LAWYERS AND SUCH. ♪

Cowboy Kids

Hanna

Cowboy Kids

Supplies

Background Cardstock:
Navy Blue, Royal Purple

Layout Cardstock:
Dark Brown, Ivory, Tan

Chalk: Dark Brown

Miniature Brads: Black

Raffia: Natural

Jute: Natural • Twine: Natural

Miniature Picket Fence

Adhesive

Journaling Marker: Black

Distressed & Aged Cardstock

- Tear a piece of cardstock into the desired shape and size. Crumple the cardstock in your hand—the tighter you crumple it the more "wrinkles" it will have.

- Unfold the crumpled cardstock and flatten it as well as possible. To age the cardstock, lightly chalk the torn edges and over each of the "wrinkle lines."

- This process can be used for making unique photo mats or as a place for journaling on your scrapbook page(s).

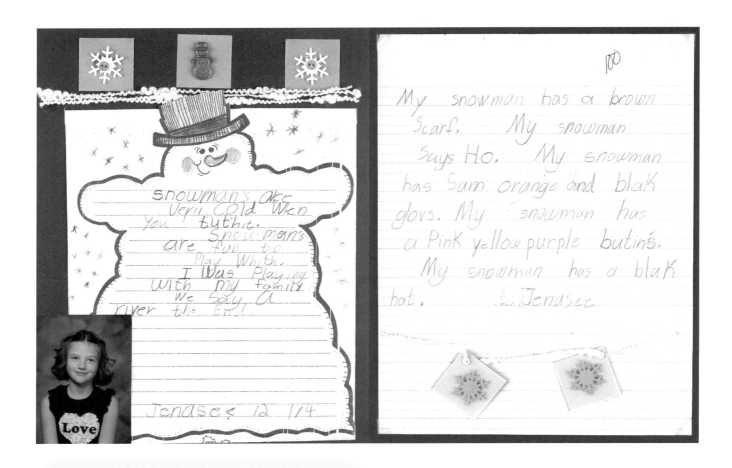

I Love Snowmen

Supplies

Background Cardstock: Navy Blue

Layout Cardstock: Periwinkle

Vellum: Clear

Photo Corners: Clear

Paper Punch: Snowflake • Buttons

Yarn: White • Snowman Charm

Hole Punch: 1/8" Diameter

Eyelets: White

Adhesive

Journaling Marker: Black

Displaying Special Schoolwork

- Position the schoolwork as desired on your scrapbook page(s).

- Place one photo corner at each corner. This allows you to be able to remove the article when desired as it is not being permanently adhered to the background cardstock.

FYI: This method is also a great way to display report cards. Keep in mind that most of these types of items are not on archival-quality papers. An archival spray that neutralizes the pH balance in the paper is available and should be used on items such as these before they are included in your scrapbook.

Rumble Young Man

Supplies

Background Cardstock:
Navy Blue

Layout Cardstock:
Red, White

Stickers:
Bumblebees, Butterfly

Embroidery Floss:
Black

Brad: Black

Adhesive

Journaling Marker:
Black

Faux-stitching Accents

- Mat your photograph(s) and/or cardstock strips, blocks, or tags.

- Draw small stitches, as evenly spaced as possible, along the outer edges of the mats. This technique draws attention to specific areas of the scrapbook page(s) without overpowering the image.

Considering Proportions

- When using images that are naturally very different in size, it is important to make them appear to have the same importance on your scrapbook page(s). In this case, a butterfly is obviously much larger than a bumblebee.

- Adhere each sticker to a piece of cardstock, then cut the cardstock into similar-sized rectangles. Because the size of the cardstock blocks is similar, both images carry the same impact.

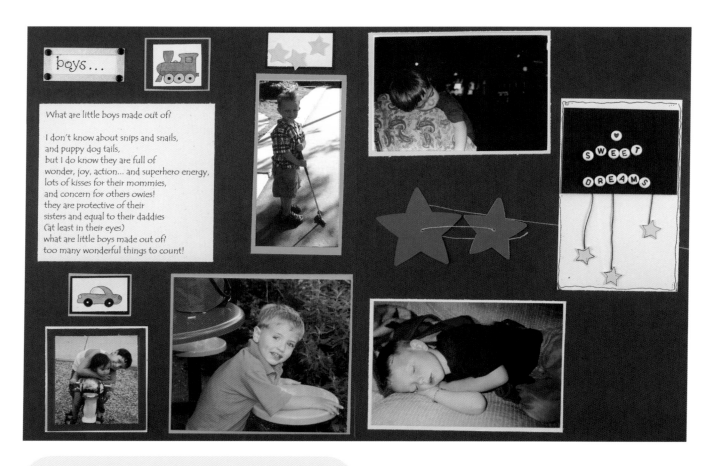

Boys . . .

Supplies

Background Cardstock: Navy Blue

Layout Cardstock: Black, Dark Brown, Mustard, Tan, Recycled White, Yellow

Metal Frame: Silver-toned

Miniature Brads: Black • Beads: Heart, Letters

Paper Punch: Small Star

Stickers: Transportation

Hole Punch: 1/8" Diameter • Rusty Stars

Embroidery Flosses: Black, Off-white

Adhesive • Journaling Marker: Black

Glued-bead Embellishment

• Position the beads as desired. Secure them in position with scrapbook glue.

Rustic Shape Embellishment

• Punch a hole in the rustic shape to accommodate the embroidery floss.

• Thread the embroidery floss through the hole(s) and wrap the excess around the shapes as desired.

FYI: Rustic shapes are available in a number of wonderful designs. Many of the shapes come in varied sizes as well. Because holes can easily be punched in them, it is very easy to incorporate them into any scrapbook page theme. Attaching them to your scrapbook page(s) can be done with adhesive, with embroidery floss, jute, or raffia, or with miniature brads.

Live, Laugh, Love

Supplies

Background Cardstock: Navy Blue

Layout Cardstock: Dark Brown, Olive Green, Brick Red, Rust, Tan

Vellum: Clear • Mesh: Rust

Metal-rimmed Tag, Rectangle: Blue

Miniature Brads: Black

Precut Tags: Kraft Paper • Pewter Letter Blocks

Stickers: Letters & Numbers

Rusty Stars

Strings: Blue, Red, Tan

Adhesive • Journaling Marker: Black

Precut Kraft-paper Tags

- Embellish each tag with letter and/or number stickers.
- If desired, tear the bottom of each tag to the desired size.
- Adhere tags in place on your scrapbook page(s).
- To add interest and dimension, combine various colors of string and thread them through the reinforced holes in the tags. Trim the ends as desired.

Pewter Letter-block Embellishment

- Position the pewter letter blocks as desired. Secure them in place with scrapbook glue.

Don't Forget How Special You Are

Supplies

Background Cardstock: Kraft

Layout Cardstock: Brown, Brick Red, Tan

Hole Punches: $1/8$" Diameter, $1/4$" Diameter

Pewter Word Blocks • Raffia: Natural • Adhesive

Journaling Markers: Assorted Colors

Pewter Word-block Embellishment

- Position the pewter word blocks as desired. Secure them in place with scrapbook glue.

FYI: These pewter word blocks are available in several different sentiments.

Matting Pewter Word Blocks

- Adhere each pewter word block to a scrap of cardstock.

- Trim the cardstock around the pewter word block to the desired height and width.

Sentiment Phrasing

- Write a different sentiment on several separate scraps of cardstock.

- Trim the cardstock around the phrases as desired and adhere in place on your scrapbook page(s).

Buggy for Bugs

Supplies

Background Cardstock:
Yellow

Layout Cardstock:
Lime Green, Periwinkle, Pink, White

Stickers:
Bug Assortment, Letters

Adhesive

Journaling Marker: Black

Sticker Tiles

- Place the stickers on the white cardstock, leaving an adequate amount of space in between each sticker.

- Cut each tile in a square or rectangular shape, centering the sticker inside the tile.

- Adhere each sticker tile to an appropriately sized piece of color-coordinated cardstock. Carefully cut the cardstock around the sticker tile, keeping the same border width around all sides.

- Randomly position the sticker tiles on your scrapbook page(s).

Word Tiles

- Place alphabet letter stickers in word form on cardstock. Repeat the process described above to make individual word tiles.

Bring on the Sun

Supplies

Background Cardstock: Lemon Yellow

Layout Cardstock: Lime Green, Purple, Lemon Yellow

Stickers: Letters, Summer Assortment

Die-cut Tags: Lime Green, Yellow

Metal-rimmed Tags, Assorted Shapes:
Lime Green, Purple

Embroidery Flosses: Green, Yellow

Paper Punches: Small Flowers, Large Spiral

Button: Yellow • Hole Punch: $^1/_8$" Diameter

Eyelets: Green, Purple, Yellow

Adhesive • Journaling Marker: Black

Combining Geometric Shapes

- Combining several different geometric shapes is a great way to add interest to your scrapbook page(s). In this case, squares, rectangles, triangles, and circles were used.

- To further enhance the geometric shapes, some were embellished with stickers, paperpunch images, die-cut and metal-rimmed tags, and even a button.

- An important element on these particular scrapbook pages is the use of bright contrasting colors. Cutting the various geometric shapes from each of the bold colors of cardstock adds excitement and makes your scrapbook page(s) busy, but fun.

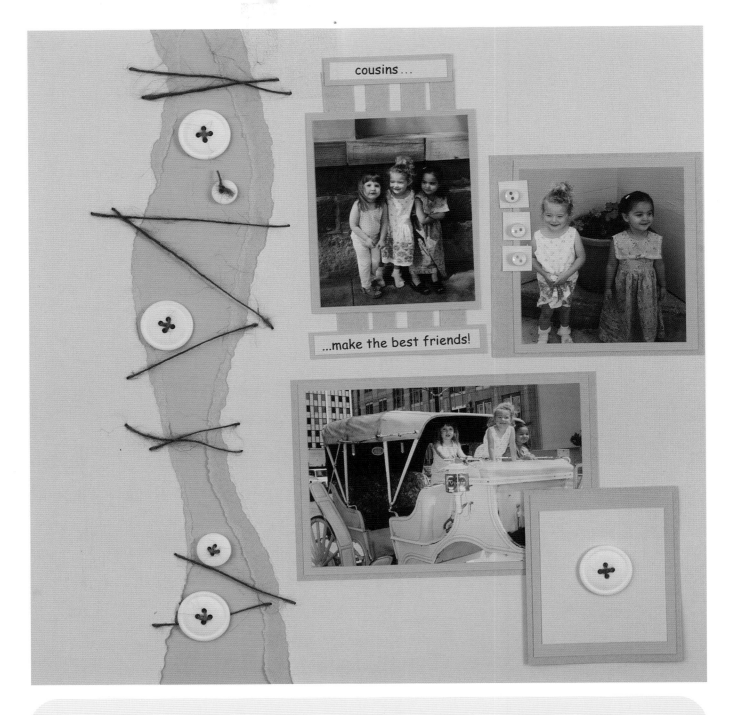

cousins...

...make the best friends!

Cousins Make the Best Friends

Supplies
Background Cardstock: Pea Green, Pastel Pink
Layout Cardstock: Pea Green, Lavender, Pastel Pink,
Buttons: White • Jute: Dark Olive Green
Adhesive
Journaling Marker: Black

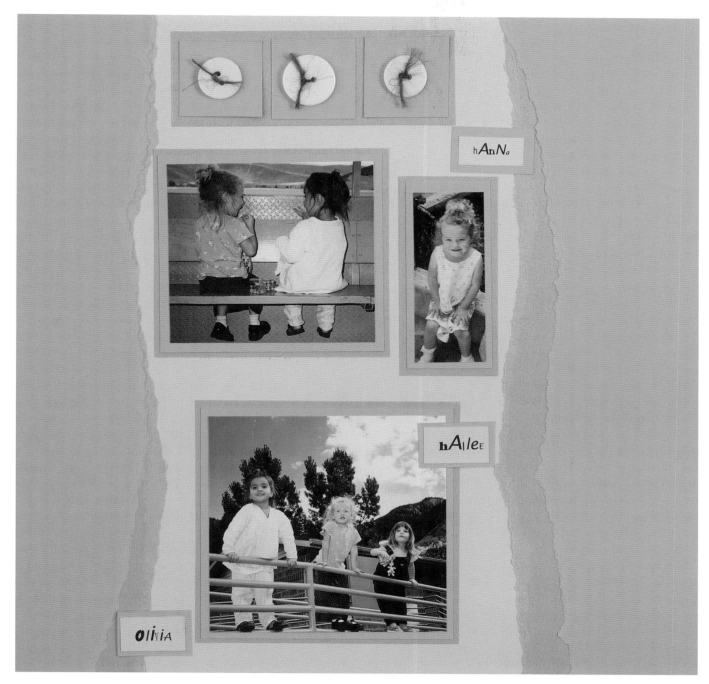

Sewn-button Embellishment

- Position the buttons as desired.

- Using a needle threaded with jute, sew on each button. Tie the jute ends into a knot to secure.

Matted Panel of Buttons

- Cut a rectangular panel from the cardstock to the desired size. Determine the length of the panel by considering the number of buttons you will be using.

- Cut one square from a contrasting color of card-stock to accommodate the size of each button.

- Center each button on each cardstock square and sew in place. Tie the jute ends into a knot to secure and trim to different lengths. Adhere each button-embellished square onto the cardstock panel as desired.

Grandma's Sweater

Supplies

Background Cardstock: Sky Blue

Layout Cardstock: Blue, White

Vellum: Clear Snowflake-embossed

Die-cuts: Snowflakes

Hole Punches: $1/4$" Diameter

Silk Ribbon, $1^1/2$" Wide: Light Blue

Yarn: White • Adhesive

Journaling Markers: Assorted Colors

Threaded-ribbon Embellishment

- Layer the background cardstock and the vellum. Punch holes into both as desired to accommodate the ribbon.

- Randomly tie the ribbon into knots. Starting and ending at the back side of the cardstock, thread the ribbon through the punched holes.

- Secure the ribbon ends at the back side of the cardstock.

Wound-yarn Embellishment

- Wind the yarn around the cardstock mat.

- Tie the yarn ends into a knot to secure.

- For enhanced texture, add additional lengths of yarn tied into knots.

Bunny Ears

Supplies

Background Cardstock: Vanilla

Layout Cardstock: Bright Pink, Pastel Pink, White

Patterned Cardstock:
Red & Off-white Plaid

Precut Tag: White

Silk Ribbon, 1¹/₂" Wide: Soft Rose

Jewels: Pink

Chalk: Pink

Adhesive

Journaling Markers: Assorted Colors

Chalking

- The use of colored chalk is a wonderful way to define an area or subject. In this case, pink chalk was used along the torn edges of the bunny ears. The bunny ears were torn from white cardstock, so the pink chalk highlights the outside perimeter of each ear. The inner ears, torn from pastel pink cardstock, were also accented with pink chalk that was applied a little darker than around the outer ears.

FYI: Chalks are available in a wonderful array of colors and are easily applied with a sponge- or cotton-type swab or with your finger. Several manufacturers combine chalks into palettes of colors for each season. For example, the color palette for Spring would include soft colors that could be found in a fresh bouquet of flowers. The colors for Fall would include rich earth tones such as browns, golds, and rich shades of red.

It's a
Grandma Thing

Supplies

Background Cardstock: Dark Brown

Layout Cardstock: Navy Blue, Goldenrod, Forest Green, Moss Green, Olive Green, Rust, Tan

Photo Corners: Kraft Paper

Silk Ribbon, 3" Wide: Variegated Brown/Green

Craft Wire: 24-gauge Silver-toned

Decorative Button • Heart-shaped Locket

Foam Dots • Adhesive

Journaling Markers: Assorted Colors

Adding Dimension with Foam Dots

- Place a couple of foam dots underneath the item(s) you want accentuated to simply "lift" the item(s) off the surface of the background. A single foam dot is approximately 1/8" thick, so the result is slight, but effective.

- If a more dramatic effect is desired, combine two foam dots together to double the amount of lift.

Heirloom Embellishment

- An heirloom, as simple as a single button from one of your grandmother's favorite dresses, makes a treasured embellishment for your scrapbook page(s).

- Other appropriate heirlooms to use on your scrapbook page(s) might include a hairpin, a piece of jewelry, or a vintage handkerchief.

Handwritten on layout:

When grandpa first held you, he didn't quite remember how, he kept saying

"What is wrong with it's Neck?"

1997

1998

1999

Grandpa

It's a Grandpa Thing

Supplies

Background Cardstock: Tan, Off-white

Layout Cardstock: Steel Blue, Brown, Dark Brown, Olive Green, Rust

Vellum: Brown • Embroidery Floss: Gray

Brad: Black • Miniature Brads: Black, Copper

Button • Pewter Stars • Paper Clip: Gold-toned

Foam Dots • Adhesive

Journaling Marker: Black

Patchwork & Embellished Hand-cut Tag

- Cut one tag from cardstock, then angle the corners at one end.

- Cut several rectangles and squares from contrasting colors of cardstock. Keep in mind that the size of the rectangles and squares must be in proportion to the size of the tag you will be covering.

- In a patchwork manner, adhere each rectangle and square in place on the cardstock tag. Don't worry if the shapes are not perfectly straight on the tag—some unevenness makes the effect look more handmade.

- Add additional embellishments to the cardstock tag, such as brads, buttons, and/or pewter shapes.

- If desired, write a special word or sentiment on one or more of the patchwork shapes.

Puppy Love

Supplies

Background Cardstock: Dark Chocolate, Tan

Layout Cardstock: Light Blue, Forest Green, Olive Green, Kraft, Tan • Mesh: Green

Paper Punch: Feet • Rusty Star • Chalk: Blue, Brown • Pewter Letter Blocks

Stickers: Letters • Sealed Bag of Sand • Precut Tags: Kraft Paper, White • Buttons

Raffia: Natural • Jute: Natural • Adhesive • Journaling Marker: Black

Torn-paper Horizons

- Tear light blue cardstock into one or more pieces to make the sky.

- Tear tan cardstock into one or more pieces to make the beach.

- Layer the pieces of blue cardstock as desired and secure in place along the top of the background cardstock. Make certain the left and right edges align with the background cardstock. Accent the torn edges with blue chalk.

- Layer the pieces of tan cardstock as desired and secure in place along the bottom of the background cardstock. Make certain the left and right edges align with the background cardstock. Accent the torn edges with brown chalk.

big fat snowflakes on my tongue

gifts

hot buttered popcorn

Christmas time favorites

THE TREE

santa

Christmas Time Favorites

Supplies

Background Cardstock: Recycled Dark Red

Layout Cardstock: Black, Brown, Olive Green, Kraft, Christmas Red, Tan, White, Recycled White, Yellow

Handmade Papers: Red, White • Paper Punches: Clouds • Chalk: Brown

Stickers: Letters • Paper Ribbon: Green • Embroidery Floss: White

Adhesive • Journaling Marker: Black

Paper-ribbon Art

- Cut the paper ribbon into appropriate widths and lengths for the art you are creating. In this case, the branches on the Christmas tree are made from green paper ribbon.

- Secure the paper-ribbon strips in place as desired. Because paper ribbon has a "crinkled" look, instant texture is added to your scrapbook page(s).

- Additional strips of paper ribbon can be added behind matted photographs for added dimension.

Five Generations of Strong Women

Supplies

Background Cardstock: Goldenrod

Layout Cardstock: Black, Dark Steel Blue, Brown, Olive Green, Kraft

Vellum: Brown, Clear, Green

Paper Punch: Medium Square • Stickers: Hearts

Photo Corners: Black • Jute: Natural

Silk Ribbon, 1/4" Wide: Brown

Adhesive

Journaling Markers: Assorted Colors

Vellum Windows

- Tear a piece of cardstock into several various-sized and -shaped pieces. Make certain all four sides have a torn edge.

- Punch one square into each of the torn cardstock shapes. When punching the squares, keep in mind that the squares do not all have to be positioned at the centers of the shapes.

- Adhere a scrap of vellum to the back side of each torn cardstock shape, making certain the vellum completely covers the square opening.

- Determine the placement of each cardstock shape and adhere a heart sticker to the background cardstock. Secure the cardstock shape to your scrapbook page(s) so each heart shows through a vellum window.

- Personalize each cardstock shape by writing above, below, or to the side of each vellum window.

Tea for Two

Supplies

Background Cardstock: Goldenrod

Layout Cardstock:
Black, Navy Blue, Olive Green, Recycled White

Die-cut Tags: Sky Blue, Lime Green, White

Vellum: Clear, Green

Paper Punches: Alphabet

Stickers: Flowers

Strings: Green, White

Adhesive

Journaling Marker: Black

Die-cut Tag Tea Bags

- Embellish one side of each die-cut tag. In this case, the letters T, E, and A were punched from black cardstock. One letter was glued to each white die-cut tag. The additional die-cut tags were embellished with flower stickers and torn-paper art.

- Cut a rectangular-shaped strip from the clear vellum. The height of the vellum strip should be equal to the height of the die-cut tag excluding the decorative die-cut upper portion which contains the hole. The length of the vellum strip should be long enough to wrap around the front side of the die-cut tag and be secured on the back side.

FYI: Most die-cut tags come with a short length of string that has been threaded through the hole and knotted at the top. If desired, this string can be replaced with a longer length of string, colored string, embroidery floss, jute, or raffia.

My Valentine

Supplies

Background Cardstock: Bright Red

Layout Cardstock: Off-white

Metal-rimmed Tags, Square: Clear Vellum

Miniature Brads: Gold-toned

Vellum: Clear

Stickers: Letters & Numbers

Heart-shaped Buttons: Gold

Mesh: White

Adhesive

Journaling Marker: Black

Metal-rimmed Vellum Tags

- Embellish each tag with number and/or letter stickers in word form or a small cluster of heart-shaped buttons.

- Attach the tags to your scrapbook page(s) with miniature brads.

Vellum-matted Mesh

- Adhere the vellum to the background cardstock as desired.

- Layer the mesh on top of the vellum and secure in place.

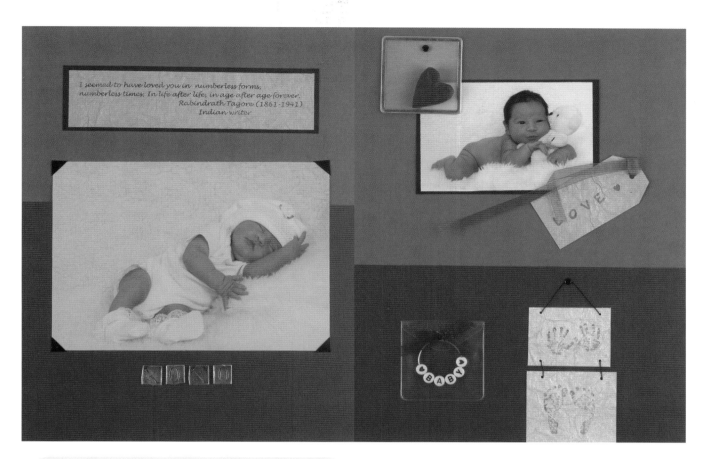

Baby Love

Supplies

Background Cardstock: Olive Green

Layout Cardstock: Black, Dark Red, Metallic Silver

Metal-rimmed Tag, Square: Clear Vellum

Photo Corners: Black • Primitive Wooden Heart

Miniature Brads: Black • Embroidery Floss: Black

Memorabilia Pocket • Baby Bracelet

Silk Ribbon, $1/4$" Wide: Dark Red

Rubber Stamps:
Alphabet, Footprints, Handprints, Small Heart

Stamp Pad: Black • Pewter Letter Blocks

Adhesive • Journaling Marker: Black

Hanging Ladder Signs

- Push the post at the back of each miniature brad through the background cardstock, then flatten out each side of the post at the back side of the background cardstock to secure.

- Punch one hole into each top corner of the upper portions of the signs you want to hang. Thread embroidery floss through the holes and tie the floss ends into a knot to secure.

- Punch one hole into each bottom corner of the upper portion of the sign. Punch one hole into each top corner of the lower portion of the sign. Thread embroidery floss through the holes in a vertical manner, allowing an adequate amount of floss for the amount of space you desire between your signs, and tie the floss ends into a knot to secure.

- Wrap the floss loop on each sign around one brad to make the sign appear to be hanging.

Sisters

Supplies

Background Cardstock: Khaki Green

Layout Cardstock: Recycled White

Vellum: Clear

Miniature Brads: Gold-toned

Metal-rimmed Tags, Rectangle: White

Hole Punch: $1/16$" Diameter

Embroidery Floss: Black

Adhesive

Journaling Markers: Assorted Colors

Vellum Pocket

- Cut a piece of vellum the width of your background cardstock. The height of the vellum should be determined by the the item(s) that is to be placed inside the pocket.

- Secure the piece of vellum to the background cardstock with miniature brads. The number of brads needed will depend on how small the item(s) is that is to be placed inside the pocket.

- Because the vellum is clear, the item(s) placed inside the pocket can also be nicely displayed.

FYI: If the item(s) being stored in the pocket is extremely delicate and you do not want someone removing the contents of the pocket, feel free to make the pocket taller than the item(s). This allows the viewer to see the entire contents without having the need to remove them.

Sisters & Friends

Supplies

Background Cardstock:
Dark Chocolate, Khaki Green

Layout Cardstock: Brown, Khaki Green, Rust

Miniature Brads: Black

Buttons: Black

Wooden Shapes: Heart, Moon

Beads: Heart, Letters

Hole Punch: $^1/_8$" Diameter

Craft Wire: 24-gauge Black

Adhesive • Journaling Marker: Black

Wire-wrapped Wooden Shapes

- Randomly wrap craft wire around wooden shapes as desired. In this case, the heart was wrapped at the center in a crisscross manner. The moon was wrapped several times around the contour of the shape.

- Adhere the wire-wrapped wooden shapes to your scrapbook page(s). In this case, the shapes were used to embellish hand-cut tags.

Curling Craft Wire

- Thread a length of craft wire through the hole at the top of a tag.

- Tightly wrap each wire end around a pencil. Carefully pull the pencil out of the wire and position the curled wire as desired.

GRADUATION 2000

Marissa Joy Mack

SENIORS

High School Graduation

Supplies

Background Cardstock: Navy Blue

Layout Cardstock: Black

Vellum: Clear

Miniature Brads: Black

Paper Punches:
Alphabet & Numbers

Miniature Graduation Cap & Diploma

Adhesive

Journaling Marker: Black

Placing Photographs on an Angle

- Position one or more matted photographs on an angle on your scrapbook page(s). Adhere in place on the background cardstock.

- If desired, a matted journaling block or tag can be placed on the background cardstock, slightly overlapping the photograph.

Using School Colors on Page Layouts

- This is the perfect example of using the traditional school colors as the background cardstock and layout cardstock colors for your scrapbook page(s). In this case, the high school colors are black and navy blue, which coordinates with the overall color palette chosen.

Preschool Graduation

Supplies

Background Cardstock: Dark Blue

Layout Cardstock: Metallic Silver

Patterned Handmade Paper:
Navy Blue with Tiny Silver Stars

Paper Punches: Numbers, Star • Bead

Hole Punch: $1/8$" Diameter

Craft Wire: 24-gauge Silver-toned

Adhesive

Journaling Marker: Black

Concealing the Corner of a Photograph

- Adhere your matted photograph(s) to the background cardstock.

- Position the layout cardstock or handmade paper, with cut or torn edges, over the corner of one or more of your photographs.

Wire-strung Punched Images

- Punch the desired number of images from a single color of the cardstock.

- Punch a hole at the center of each image to accommodate the craft wire.

- Thread a length of wire through the holes and curl the wire ends around a pencil. Remove the pencil and flatten the wire against the background cardstock. Adhere the images in place.

Happy Campers

Supplies

Background Cardstock: Brown

Layout Cardstock: Dark Brown, Recycled Buckskin, Olive Green, Dark Olive Green, Mustard, Rust

Vellum: Brown • Tree Brads • Wooden Carrot Button

Jute: Green, Natural • Raffia: Natural

Adhesive • Journaling Marker: Black

Dimensional Photo Mats

- Adhere each photograph onto an appropriately sized piece of cardstock. Carefully cut the cardstock around the photograph, differing the border width around all sides.

- Add one or more pieces of coordinating or contrasting cardstock. Mat widths should vary with each layer and at least one side of each mat should be considerably shorter than the previous mat for added dimension.

- When matting your photographs, leave a nice wide border on the left side of the photographs so torn-vellum strips can be added. Further embellish each strip with shaped brads, torn cardstock, and/or lengths of raffia.

aunt APRIL
things I love about Aunt April...
loves me lots and lots
takes time to make me her special girl...
takes me to the zoo when she is in town
tells me how special I am
sends me packages for special occasions
reads me lots of books
April is really your cousin, but when you were just a baby she fell head over heels in love with you, and insisted that I refer to her as Aunt April to you...so that is what you know her as!

My Favorite Aunt

Supplies

Background Cardstock: Gray

Layout Cardstock: Black, Gray, Forest Green

Miniature Brads: Black

Charms: Stars with Moon Insets

Embroidery Floss: Black

Stickers: Letters

Adhesive

Journaling Marker: Black

Vertical Journaling Strips

- Cut several strips from the cardstock. Keep the strips approximately the same height, but vary the lengths depending on the sentiment you want to write on each strip.
- Write a separate sentiment on each strip.
- Cut a single strip from a contrasting color of cardstock and attach it to your scrapbook page(s) in a horizontal manner with one miniature brad at placed each side.
- Adhere the cardstock sentiment strips in a vertical manner over the horizontal cardstock strip. Vary the position of each of the sentiment strips to add interest.

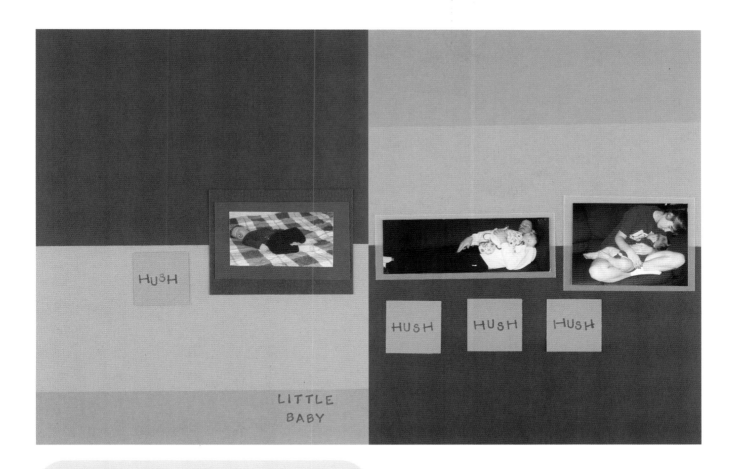

Hush Little Baby

Supplies

Background Cardstock: Gray

Layout Cardstock:
Dark Brown, Forest Green, Kraft

Vellum: Clear

Paper Punch: 1" Square

Rubber Stamps:
Uppercase Alphabet

Stamp Pad: Black

Adhesive

Journaling Marker: Black

Repetitious Journaling Blocks

- Punch several blocks from the cardstock.

- Position the desired number in a horizontal or vertical row and adhere in place. Make certain to keep the blocks as evenly spaced as possible.

- Stamp the desired sentiment on each cardstock block. In this case, all of the blocks have the same stamped sentiment to provide repetition to the theme of the scrapbook pages.

Using a Single Photograph

- Occasionally a single photograph will be strong enough to carry the theme of your scrapbook page(s). In this case, the photograph of the sleeping child is perfect for the "Hush Little Baby" theme.

Spook Party

Supplies

Background Cardstock: Purple

Layout Cardstock: Black, Kraft, Purple, White

Patterned Vellums: Moon & Stars, Spider Webs

Stickers:
Halloween Assortment; Letters & Numbers

Die Cut: Witch's Cauldron

Metal-rimmed Tag, Square: Clear Vellum

Hole Punches: 1/8" Diameter; 1/4" Diameter

Eyelets: Black • String: White

Chalk: Gray • Ultrafine Glitter: Mint

Adhesive • Journaling Marker: Black

Glitter Embellishment

- Lightly apply scrapbook glue to the area of the scrapbook page(s) that you want to accent with glitter. In this case, the steaming "brew" coming out of the witch's cauldron.

- Generously sprinkle ultrafine glitter onto the glue and let the glue dry. Tap the scrapbook page on its side onto a clean scrap sheet of paper to remove the excess glitter.

- Return the excess to its container for use in the future.

Halloween

Supplies

Background Cardstock: Purple

Layout Cardstock: Black, Kraft, Mustard

Vellum: Brown

Charms: Bats, Broom, Ghosts, Pumpkin, Tombstone

Embroidery Floss: Black

Paper Punches: $1^{1}/_{2}$" Square, $^{3}/_{4}$" Square

Miniature Brad: Copper

Stencil: $^{1}/_{2}$" Square Checkerboard

Stamp Pad: Black • Sponge Dauber

Adhesive • Journaling Marker: Black

Stenciling Page Borders

- Position the checkerboard stencil along the edge of the background cardstock you want to stencil. If necessary, secure with tape so it cannot move.

- Saturate the sponge dauber with black ink from the stamp pad. Beginning with the left side of the stencil, carefully begin pouncing the dauber over each opening on the stencil. When the ink begins to fade, reload the dauber with more ink. Continue until the checkerboard pattern is complete. Let the ink dry.

- Carefully remove the tape and the stencil.

- Repeat the process on any other sides of the scrapbook page(s) you want to stencil.

spring

summer

All Four Seasons

Supplies

Background Cardstock: Navy Blue, Goldenrod

Layout Cardstock: Assorted Colors • Vellum: Clear • Sticker: Dragonfly

Paper Punches: Seasonal Assortment, Small- to Medium-sized

Miniature Brads: Black • Yarn: White • String: Blue • Raffia: Natural

Miniature Clothespins • Hole Punch: 1/8" Diameter • Eyelets: Black

Craft Wire: 24-gauge Black • Adhesive • Journaling Marker: Black

Clothesline with Miniature Clothespins

- Set one eyelet at each side of the background cardstock. Starting and ending at the back side of the cardstock, thread wire through one eyelet, through the tiny hole at the center of each miniature clothespin, then through the remaining eyelet. Twist the wire ends at the back side of the background cardstock to secure.

- Cut several squares or rectangles from various colors of cardstock, then mat each one with a contrasting color of cardstock.

- Embellish with punched images or stickers, then hang from the wire with miniature clothespins. Glue each clothespin into place with scrapbook glue.

Country Girls

Supplies

Background Cardstock:
Moss Green

Layout Cardstock: Brown, Mustard

Precut Tag: Kraft Paper

Raffia: Natural

Jute: Blue

Chalk: Brown

Lasered Die Cuts: Wheat

Adhesive

Journaling Marker: Black

Checkerboard Backgrounds

- Cut one sheet of cardstock into four equal-sized pieces. One $8^1/_2$" x 11" sheet divides into four $4^1/_4$" x 5" pieces. This can easily be done by cutting the original sheet of cardstock in half vertically, then in half horizontally.

- Adhere each piece onto the background cardstock in a kitty-corner manner, aligning them along the horizontal and vertical sides of each sheet of background cardstock.

Laser-cut Die-cut Embellishment

- Lasered die cuts are extremely delicate because of the intricacy of their designs. Take care when adhering them to your scrapbook page(s).

FYI: Lasered die cuts are extraordinary decorative elements to use on your scrapbook page(s). Hundreds of designs are available, including words and phrases.

Stay Curious

Supplies

Background Cardstock:
Stonewashed Blue

Layout Cardstock: Brown, Dark Brown,
Olive Green, Dark Kraft, Tan

Sheet Protector

Miniature Brads: Black, Copper

Pewter Word Block

Craft Wire: 24-gauge Brown

Dried Wheat

Adhesive

Journaling Marker: Black

Shaker Window Embellishment

- Cut two pieces from two different colors of cardstock exactly the same size.

- Cut one piece to that exact size from a sheet protector or piece of acetate.

- Adhere one of the pieces of cardstock to your scrapbook page. Place double-sided foam tape around the outside edges of this piece of cardstock. Place dried wheat inside opening, then adhere the piece of sheet protector on top of the foam tape to enclose the wheat.

- Gently shake the scrapbook page to allow the wheat to shake freely inside the window.

- Tear the remaining piece of cardstock horizontally and vertically to create four strips with torn inner edges. Adhere in place to create a border around the window.

Roses Are Red

Supplies

Background Cardstock:
Dark Red

Layout Cardstock: Black, Tan

Vellum: Clear

Stickers: Roses

Hole Punch: $1/8$" Diameter

Eyelets: Black

Adhesive

Journaling Markers:
Assorted Colors

Adding Drama with Black Cardstock

- Mat the main elements of your scrapbook page(s) with black cardstock.

- Add a wide vertical strip down the left-hand side of one scrapbook page.

- Cut several narrow strips in varying lengths from black cardstock.

- Position each series of cardstock strips in a horizontal and/or vertical format spaced approximately $1/4$" apart. In this case, both horizontal and vertical strips were used.

- Attach a piece of vellum over the series of black cardstock strips with one eyelet positioned at each corner.

Words of Wisdom,
Never underestimate the comforts of:
    LOVE
    SHOES
    and CHOCOLATE
                 (not necessarily in that order)

I Love Chocolate

Supplies

Background Cardstock: Kraft

Layout Cardstock: Dark Brown, Red, Tan

Paper Punch:
Small Heart, Small High-heeled Shoe

Photo Overlay: Dark Brown

Chocolate Bars

Miniature Brad: Gold-toned

Rhinestone & Pearl

Adhesive

Journaling Marker: Black

Photo Overlay Tic-Tac-Toe Board

- Remove the precut squares from the photo overlay and clean up any cardstock "burrs" along the edges.

- Save the precut squares to use as a decorative element on these scrapbook pages or for use in the future.

- Adhere the photo overlay onto the background cardstock.

- Randomly place punched images and/or other items inside some of the openings.

- If desired, embellish the precut squares with additional punched images. In this case, the high-heeled shoes were adhered to the center of each precut square, then embellished with a miniature brad, a rhinestone, and a pearl.

We Miss You

Kiara
Emma
Bird

Special Little Angel

Supplies

Background Cardstock: Pastel Pink • Patterned Vellum: Florals

Layout Cardstock: Olive Green, Hot Pink, White

Silk Ribbons, 1" Wide: Cranberry, Moss Green, Light Pink

Metal-rimmed Tags, Square: Clear Vellum • Embroidery Floss: Pink

Hole Punch: $1/8$" Diameter • Dangle Hearts • Assorted Beads • Button

Pewter Word Blocks • Adhesive • Journaling Markers: Assorted Colors

Heart Dangle Embellishments

- Punch a series of evenly spaced holes along the bottom of a matted photograph.

- Insert the wire hangers on the appropriate number of hearts through the holes at the bottom of the photo mat and crimp the wires to secure.

- Thread embroidery floss through the wire hangers on the number of hearts desired. Begin stitching with the embroidery floss onto the background cardstock in a decorative manner, allowing the hearts to dangle freely. Secure in place with scrapbook glue.

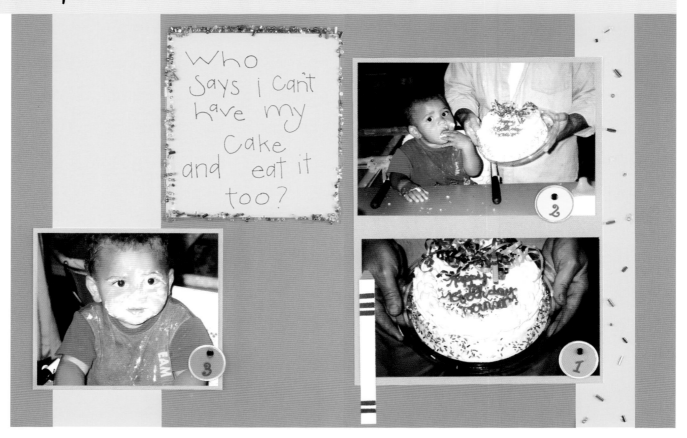

Who Says I Can't Have My Cake & Eat It Too?

Supplies

Background Cardstock: Red

Layout Cardstock: Blue, White, Yellow

Multicolored Beads

Metal-rimmed Tags, Small Circles:
Blue, Turquoise, Yellow

Stickers: Numbers • Miniature Brads: Black

Adhesive • Journaling Marker: Black

Number Sequencing on Photographs

- Adhere one metal-rimmed tag to each photograph with miniature brads.

- In numerical sequence, place a number sticker on each tag.

Multicolored-bead Embellishment

- Randomly position multicolored beads onto your scrapbook page(s) as desired. Adhere in place with scrapbook glue. The beads can be applied in a heavy application or very sparsely scattered depending on the effect you desire.

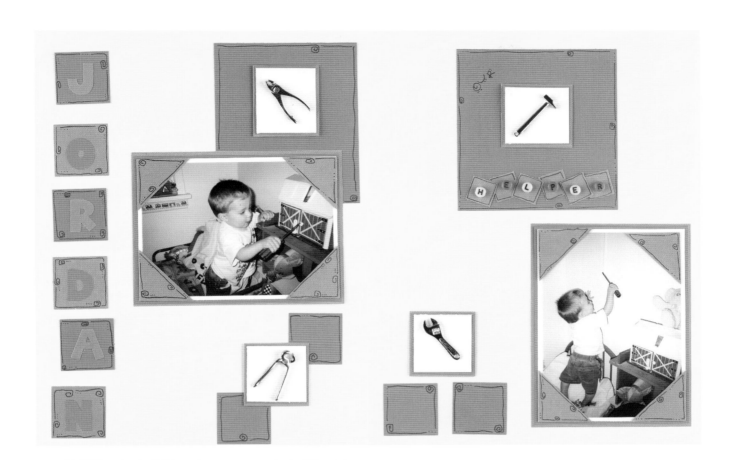

Our
Little Helper

Supplies

Background Cardstock:
Pastel Yellow

Layout Cardstock:
Blue, Red, White

Beads: Letters

Miniature Tools

Adhesive

Journaling Marker: Black

Cardstock Photo Corners

- Cut several squares from the cardstock. All of the squares must be the exact same size.

- Cut each of the squares in half diagonally to make two triangles.

- Draw the same design around the outer edges of each of the cardstock triangles.

- Adhere one triangle to each corner of the photograph, aligning them along the horizontal and vertical sides of each photograph.

Embellishing with Miniatures

- Mat and dhere the miniatures to your scrapbook page(s) with scrapbook glue. In this case, miniature tools were added to tie in with the theme of the scrapbook pages.

Visions of Sugarplums

Supplies

Background Cardstock: Light Olive Green

Layout Cardstock: Black, Brown, Dark Brown, Burgundy, Olive Green, Kraft, Mustard, Red, White

Paper Punches: Cloud, Large Spiral

Hole Punches: $1/8$" Diameter, $1/4$" Diameter

Multicolored Beads • Pearls • Snow • Stocking

Star Brad • Leather Cord: Black • String: White

Gingerbread Ladies • Soldier • Plastic Envelope

Snowflake Eyelet: White • Adhesive

Journaling Markers: Assorted Colors

Transforming Paper-punch Images

To make a Candy Cane:

- Punch one large spiral from white cardstock. Position it on a scrap of white cardstock and trim it as necessary.

- Draw the pink stripes on the candy cane.

To make Popcorn:

- Punch several clouds from white cardstock. Randomly space and position each cloud on the string as though popcorn was being strung.

To make Cranberries:

- Punch several dots with the $1/4$"-diameter paper punch from dark red cardstock. Randomly space and position each dot on the string as though cranberries were being strung.

Gone Fishin'

Supplies

Background Cardstock: Light Olive Green

Layout Cardstock:
Dark Steel Blue, Dark Khaki, Mustard

Memorabilia Pocket • Fishing Hook • Dried Twig

Embroidery Floss: Off-white

Miniature Clothespin • Raffia: Natural

Hole Punch: $1/8$" Diameter • Eyelet: Black

Craft Wire: 24-gauge Brown

Adhesive • Journaling Marker: Black

Twig Fishing Pole

- Find a dried twig that is an appropriate size for using on your scrapbook page(s).

- Attach the twig to the background cardstock with lengths of craft wire spaced as necessary. Twist the craft wire on the back side of the background cardstock to secure. Avoid pulling the craft wire too tightly, the twig may break.

- Wrap embroidery floss around the top end of the twig, then allow several inches of additional floss to hang down the page. Attach a single miniature clothespin to the end of the floss.

- Place the actual fish hook in the *memorabilia pocket* and adhere to your scrapbook page(s).

Ghosts, Witches & Creepy Spiders

Supplies

Background Cardstock:
Black, Hunter's Orange

Layout Cardstock:
Black, Soft Moss Green, Hunter's Orange

Mesh: Black, Orange

Strings: Black, Off-white

3-D Spiders • Die Cut: Spiderweb

Hole Punch: $1/8$" Diameter

Colored Pencils • Adhesive

Journaling Marker: Black

String Whiskers & Hair

To make Whiskers:

- Hand-tear a black cat from the cardstock.

- Punch four holes on each side of the cat's nose.

- Cut four equal lengths from the string. Thread each length of string through the holes beginning from left to right and front to back, then back to front.

To make Hair:

- Hand-tear a witch from the cardstock.

- Punch approximately eight holes on each side of the witch's head.

- Repeat threading instructions from above.

- Place the witch's hat so the "hair" comes out from underneath.

Pretty as a Poppy

Supplies

Background Cardstock:
Dark Olive

Layout Cardstock:
Black, Tangerine

Paper Ribbon: White

Chalk: Orange

Brads: Black

Adhesive

Journaling Marker:
Black

Paper-ribbon Flowers

- Cut several individual flower petals from the paper ribbon.

- Chalk over each of the petals until you have achieved the desired amount of color.

- Cut one square or rectangle from the cardstock in which to attach each paper-ribbon flower. It is best to use a dark, contrasting color such as black so the detail of each flower is obvious.

- Layer the flower petals and place a brad at the center of each flower. Push the post at the back of each brad through the paper-ribbon petals and the cardstock, then flatten out each side of the post at the back side to secure.

River Bridge Picnic

Supplies

Background Cardstock: Kraft

Layout Cardstock: Dark Brown

Patterned Papers:
Barnwood, Brown Gingham,
Green Gingham, Pinecones

Preprinted Photo Corners & Acorn Artwork

Die Cut: Twig Frame • Alphabet Letter Stencil

Decorative Scissors: Wave-edged

Stickers: Bluebird, Branches

Adhesive • Journaling Marker: Black

Stenciled-letter Tiles

- Trace the letters from the stencil backward onto the back side of the patterned paper. Make certain to do it backward so when you turn the letter right side up it will read correctly.

- Cut out each letter, avoiding cutting out the center sections where the letters may normally have an opening.

- Adhere the letters to the cardstock, allowing plenty of cutting area around each one.

- Cut-out the letter tiles with decorative scissors, centering each letter inside each tile.

- Randomly position the letter tiles on the background cardstock.

FYI: To add dimension, place a foam dot under each letter tile.

Senior Prom

Supplies

Background Cardstock:
Dark Brown

Layout Cardstock:
Black, Gray, White

Die Cut:
Limousine

Miniature Bow Tie, Invitation, Tuxedo

Miniature Prom Dress on
Leather Tag with Wire Hanger

Adhesive

Journaling Marker:
Black

Using Card-making Miniatures

• Adhere each miniature to the background cardstock or matted rectangle with scrapbook glue.

FYI: The miniatures used on these scrapbook pages include the bow tie, tuxedo, invitation, and prom dress hanging on a leather tag. These are actually elements that are found in the card-making supplies at any craft store. Miniatures add quite a lot of dimension to your scrapbook page(s) so should be used accordingly.

A Day at the Farm

Supplies

Background Cardstock: Recycled Buckskin, Kraft

Layout Cardstock: Dark Brown, Recycled Buckskin, Forest Green, Soft Moss Green, Maize, Rust, Tan

Embroidery Floss: Green • Jute: Burgundy • Rusty Heart • Assorted Beads

Miniature Brads: Black • Hole Punches: $1/8$" Diameter, $1/4$" Diameter

Mesh: Green • Large Grid Mesh: White

Tiny Plastic Eggs • Adhesive • Journaling Markers: Assorted Colors

3-D Journaling Tags Using Raffia

- Adhere a piece of cardstock to the background cardstock.

- Position cut strands of raffia vertically on the piece of cardstock. Adhere in place with scrapbook glue.

- Write an appropriate sentiment on a contrasting color of cardstock. Adhere in place on top of the raffia with scrapbook glue.

All Boy

Supplies

Background Cardstock:
Forest Green

Layout Cardstock:
Black, Brown, White

Stickers:
Ladybug, Letters

Hole Punch: 1/4" Diameter

Leather Cord: Black

Miniature Brads: Black

Adhesive

Journaling Marker: Black

Threaded Leather-cord Embellishment

- Punch two holes horizontally in each top corner of a square of cardstock.

- Thread the leather cord, front to back, then back to front, leaving a 2" tail on the outside edge.

- Tie an overhand knot, then carry the length of the cord across the top of the cardstock square.

- Repeat the knotting process on the opposite corner.

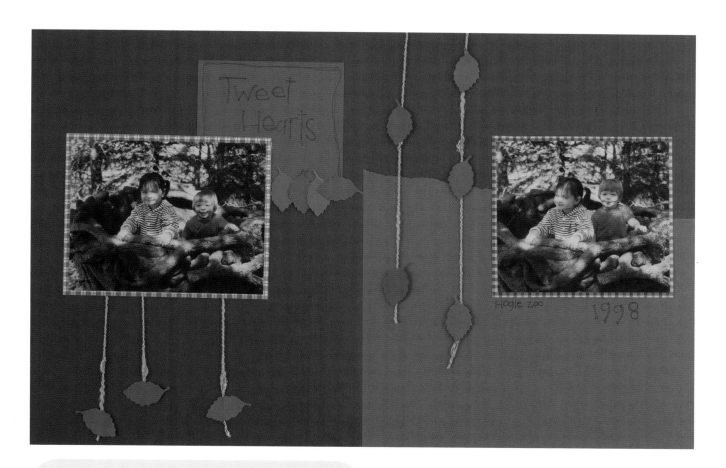

Tweet-Hearts

Supplies

Background Cardstock:
Forest Green, Pine Green

Layout Cardstock:
Brown, Dark Brown, Olive Green

Patterned Papers:
Brown & Green Checks,
Olive Green Gingham

Paper Punch: Leaf

Woven Yarn

Adhesive

Journaling Markers:
Assorted Colors

Hanging Vines

- Punch several leaves from the cardstock.

- Cut the woven yarn into various-sized lengths. Adhere the yarn in place vertically on the background cardstock.

- Randomly position the leaves on the yarn as desired. Adhere in place with scrapbook glue.

- Further embellish the background cardstock with additional leaves.

Snowman
Stareoff

Supplies

Background Cardstock: Dark Purple

Layout Cardstock: Brown, White

Vellum: Clear • Chalk: Gray

Thick Yarn: White • Kite String

Miniature Brads: Black

Buttons: Yellow

Hole Punch: $1/4$" Diameter • Eyelets: White

Foam Dots • Adhesive

Journaling Marker: Black

3-D Journaling Tags Using Thick Yarn

- Position cut strands of thick yarn vertically on the background cardstock. Adhere in place with scrapbook glue.

- Write an appropriate sentiment on a piece of vellum. Adhere in place on top of the yarn with scrapbook glue.

- To give extra support, place one foam dot under each corner of the piece of vellum.

- Punch four dots from the black cardstock and adhere on top of the vellum over the foam dots to conceal them.

Father, Brother, Son & Friend

Supplies

Background Cardstock: Dark Purple

Layout Cardstock:
Olive Green, Kraft, Dark Red

Silk Ribbon, 1 1/2" Wide: Cranberry

Hole Punch: 1/4" Diameter

Star Charm • Jute: Red

Paper Punches: Alphabet, Star

Adhesive

Journaling Markers: Assorted Colors

Jute-strung Alphabet Letters

- Punch the appropriate letters to spell the phrase or sentiment you desire from a single color of the cardstock. Make certain each of the letters you are using has an opening in them to accommodate the jute. For example, the letters C, E, F, G, H, I, J, K, L, M, N, S, T, U, V, W, X, Y and Z will not work for this technique.

- Thread a length of jute through the openings in each letter and secure the jute ends under matted photographs and/or journaling strips, blocks, or tags.

FYI: If desired, the letters can be glued to the jute as was done here with the stars.

Santa

Supplies

Background Cardstock: Dark Red

Layout Cardstock: Metallic Gold, Forest Green, Dark Olive Green, White

Vellum: Brown • Hole Punch: ¹/₈" Diameter • Eyelets: White • Star Brad

Stickers: Letters • Pewter Word Block • Mittens • Thick Yarn: White

Miniature Clothespins • Circular Paper Clip • Heart Charm on Ribbon

Adhesive • Journaling Markers: Assorted Colors

Matted-brad Embellishment

- Push the post at the back of each decorative brad through the cardstock, then flatten out each side of the post at the back side to secure.

- Cut the cardstock area around the brad to the desired shape and size.

- If desired, this brad embellishment can be double- and/or triple-matted for added dimension.

FYI: Decorative brads are available in many different shapes including stars, trees, flowers, and hearts. Colored brads can also be found, but most decorative brads are silver- or gold-toned.

Arches National Park

Supplies

Background Cardstock:
Steel Blue

Layout Cardstock:
Burgundy, Cinnamon, Olive Green, Ivory

Miniature Brads: Gold-toned

Chalk: Brown

Adhesive

Journaling Marker: Black

Using Enlarged Photographs

- Certain photographs deserve to be enlarged. Choose your favorites and enlarge to 5" x 7" in size. This will help fill your scrapbook page(s) nicely and gives added impact to the theme of your scrapbook page(s).

- Adhere the photographs to the background cardstock. If desired, mat your photographs first.

FYI: 5" x 7" photo enlargements work well on $8^{1}/_{2}$" x 11" and 12" x 12" scrapbook pages; 8" x 10" photo enlargements are best reserved for 12" x 12" scrapbook pages.

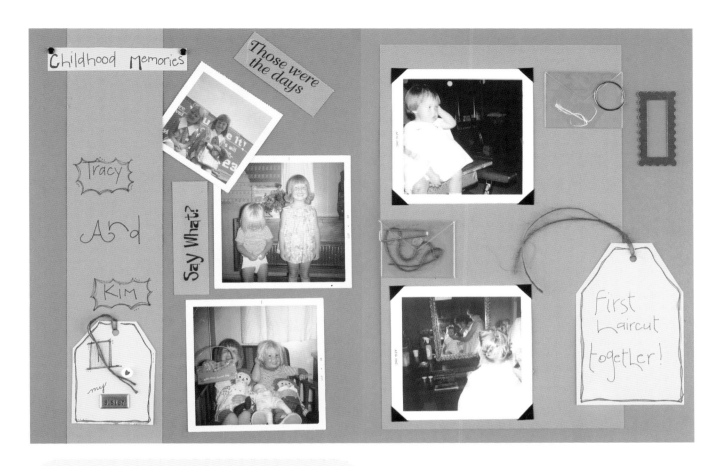

Our First Haircut Together

Supplies

Background Cardstock: Burnt Sienna

Layout Cardstock:
Goldenrod, Light Olive Green

Stickers: Phrases • Pewter Word Block

Miniature Brads: Black • Plastic Envelopes

Photo Corners: Black • Embroidery Floss: Rust

Bead: Heart • Jute: Red, White

Paper Clips • Adhesive

Journaling Markers: Assorted Colors

Using Paper Clips for Attaching Embellishments

• Use a single paper clip to secure each of the plastic envelopes to the layout cardstock. Make certain the layout cardstock has been adequately adhered to the background cardstock, yet leaving an area for the paper clip to slip under the outside edge.

FYI: Paper clips are available in decorative shapes and sizes. They can be used as a functional accessory on your pages as described above or simply as a decorative accessory.

Playground Fun

Supplies

Background Cardstock: Navy Blue

Layout Cardstock:
Green, Red, Recycled White, Yellow

Metal-rimmed Tags, Assorted Rectangles:
Green, Red, White, Yellow

Mesh: Green • Hole Punch: $1/8$" Diameter

Eyelets: Green, Red, Yellow

Paper Punch: Dog Bone • Adhesive

Journaling Markers: Assorted Colors

Primary-colored Checkerboard Background

- Cut one $4^{1}/_{4}$" x 5" piece from the green card-stock, the yellow cardstock, and the red card-stock. This can easily be done by cutting the original sheet of cardstock in half vertically, then in half horizontally.

- Adhere each piece onto the background card-stock in a kitty-corner manner, aligning them along the horizontal and vertical sides of each sheet of background cardstock.

Using Paper-punched Images for Letters

- Use paper-punched images as a substitute for alphabet letters that resemble the shape. In this case, the dog bone was used as the letter I in the name Chris.

Amusement Park Fun

Supplies

Background Cardstock:
Sky Blue

Layout Cardstock:
Black, Green, Red, Yellow

Paper Punches: Alphabet

Stickers:
Amusement Park Assortment

Adhesive

Journaling Markers:
Assorted Colors

Two-toned Letters

- Punch the appropriate letters to spell the phrase or sentiment you desire from a single color of the cardstock.

- Punch the same phrase or sentiment from a second color of the cardstock.

- Cut the letters from the second color of cardstock in half horizontally.

- Place them on top of the complete letters and adhere in place.

FYI: This technique can also be done with a third color. Another exciting option is to use a patterned paper for one half of the letters.

You're
a Natural

Supplies
Background Cardstock: Pastel Blue, Pastel Green
Layout Cardstock: Brown, Lime Green, Lavender, Yellow
Vellum: Green • Hole Punch: $1/8$" Diameter
Glass Bead: Clear • Fibers: Assorted Designs & Colors
Adhesive • Journaling Markers: Assorted Colors

Filmstrip Photo Placement

- When photographs are taken, one right after the other, the film shows a special sequence of the event.

- Display such photographs by positioning them, evenly spaced, across the top or bottom of your scrapbook page(s).

- Even when the photographs are not from any special sequence of a single event, the results from this method can be quite dramatic.

Of All
the girls
i have loved,
in My life

I Love
Mom
the Most

Supplies

Background Cardstock: Recycled Cayenne, Recycled Rust

Layout Cardstock: Goldenrod, Olive Green, Kraft

Paper Punches: $1/2$" Circle, Maple Leaf, Oak Leaf, $1/2$" Square

Hole Punch: $1/4$" Diameter

Jute: Dark Green, Natural • Burlap Cord

Adhesive • Journaling Markers: Assorted Colors

Paper-punched Windows

- Make several various-sized hand-cut tags.

- Punch one opening into each of the hand-cut tags. When punching the openings, keep in mind that the openings do not all have to be positioned at the centers of the tags. In this case, a square punch and a maple leaf punch were used for the openings on the tags.

- Adhere a scrap of cardstock, vellum, or patterned paper to the back side of each hand-cut tag, making certain the scrap completely covers the opening.

- Secure the hand-cut tags with paper-punched windows to your scrapbook page(s).

There's *No Place* Like Home

Supplies

Background Cardstock:
Soft Moss Green

Layout Cardstock:
Yellow

Microbeads: Red

Miniature Broomstick

Yarn Fiber

Adhesive

Journaling Marker:
Black

Yarn-fiber Writing

- Using the tip on the bottle of scrapbook glue, write an appropriate sentiment on your scrapbook page(s) with the glue.

- Carefully place a single length of yarn fiber over the glue along the contour of the letters. Trim the yarn fiber once you have completed the writing. Let set until glue is completely dry.

- This technique works well when writing in "cursive." When doing *manuscript* letters a separate length of yarn fiber needs to cut for each letter.

Sunflower Sweetheart

Supplies

Background Cardstock:
Recycled Putty

Layout Cardstock:
Dark Brown, Forest Green,
Soft Moss Green, Hunter's Orange, Yellow

Paper Punches:
$1/2$" Circle, Flower, Leaf

Color-tinting Kit

Adhesive

Journaling Marker:
Black

Color Tinting
Black-and-White Photographs

- Begin with a quality color copy of the photograph(s) you want to tint. Even though the original photo(s) is black-and-white, you will need to get a "color" copy so the shades of black are correct.

- Using the color-copied photograph(s), determine which areas of your photograph(s) are to be highlighted with color tint.

- Before beginning, carefully read all manufacturer's instructions that come with your color-tinting kit. Continue with the process until you have achieved the desired brightness of color.

FYI: Photographs can be accented with a single color of tint or with several different colors of tint.

Yellowstone National Park

Supplies
Background Cardstock: Recycled Buckskin
Layout Cardstock: Dark Olive Green
Vellum: Clear • Jute: Natural
Tree Brads • Fibers • Assorted Beads
Metal-rimmed Tags, Rectangle: White
Adhesive • Journaling Markers: Assorted Colors

Fiber & Bead Tassel Tag Embellishment

- Randomly thread an assortment of beads onto a length of natural fibers. Repeat until you have the number of strands desired.

- Attach the tassel to a hand-cut tag with a tree brad.

FYI: Feathers can also be added to your tassels to offer flair from the southwest. Shells can be added to your tassels to enhance your ocean-themed scrapbook page(s).

Torn-vellum Art

- Tear a piece of vellum into the shape desired. In this case, the "eruption" of a geyser.

Autumn Harvest

Supplies

Background Cardstock: Recycled Mustard

Layout Cardstock:
Navy Blue, Dark Brown, Dark Olive Green,
Light Olive Green, Ivory

Patterned Paper: Floral • Silk Ribbon, 1/2" Wide: Pink

Hole Punch: 1/4" Diameter

Assorted Buttons • Rhinestones • Fibers

Raffia: Natural • Pewter Word Blocks

Adhesive

Journaling Markers: Assorted Colors

Patchwork Page Borders

- Determine your patchwork design. In this case, the patchwork configuration was made up of rectangles and squares.

- Cut the shapes from various-colors of the cardstock. Lay out each piece to make certain the design will work, then adhere in place.

Cardstock Ribbon

- Cut a strip of cardstock to the desired width.

- Cut a "V" into each end to replicate a piece of cut ribbon.

Grandma's
Men

Supplies

Background Cardstock:
Dark Olive Green, Light Olive Green

Layout Cardstock:
Charcoal

Vellums: Blue, Clear, Gold, Tan

Miniature Brads: Black

Adhesive

Journaling Marker:
Black

Layered Vellum Strips

- Cut the vellum into horizontal strips. The strips can be the exact height or may vary depending on your preference.

- Position the vellum strips on the background cardstock, overlapping as desired.

- Secure in position by placing a miniature brad at each intersecting corner.

- Mat your photograph(s) with a dark color of cardstock to help capture the focal point of your scrapbook page(s).

- Adhere your photograph(s) as desired on top of the layered vellum strips.

*things mom always told me
about her childhood...
' she adored her mother
... if anyone told her anything,
she would look up at her mother
and say... "is it?"
...she always wished she had a
nickel for a caramel apple.
... she thought the neighbor kids were
rich because they had candy in their fridge.
...she thought her sister always
playing with paper dolls was so stupid.*

Hanna Mae Bartlett

Mom's Childhood

Supplies

Background Cardstock: Chocolate

Layout Cardstock:
Recycled Ivory

Patterned Paper: Brown Floral

Vellum: Clear

Photo Corners: Kraft Paper

Assorted Scraps of Lace • Assorted Buttons

Embroidery Floss: Ivory

Adhesive • Journaling Marker: Black

Lace Contouring

- Tear a sheet of patterned paper approximately in half along the diagonal.

- Adhere it to the background cardstock.

- Position a scrap of lace along the contour of the torn-edged paper and adhere in place with scrapbook glue.

Photo Toppers

- Embellish the top half-inch of some or all of your photographs. Use a variety of objects including scraps of patterned paper, cardstock, buttons, ribbon, embroidery floss, and lace.

FYI: This method is a great way to accent vintage photos. Using earthtone shades of cardstock and patterned paper are the best choice of color when working with sepia-toned photographs.

Here Comes Trouble

Supplies

Background Cardstock: Dark Brown

Layout Cardstock:
Lavender

Square Template

Craft Knife

Medium-tipped Permanent Markers:
Assorted Colors

Foam Dots

Adhesive

Journaling Marker: Black

Raised Photo Accent

- Determine the focal point of each of the photographs you are using on a special scrapbook page(s).

- Firmly hold the square template over that area of the photograph(s) and carefully cut around the template with a very sharp craft knife.

- Remove the part of the photograph(s) that has been cut out.

- Adhere the photograph(s) to the background cardstock.

- Place foam dots inside the opening on the photograph, then reposition the removed portion of that particular photograph on top of the foam dots.

Little League Softball

Supplies

Background Cardstock:
Forest Green

Layout Cardstock:
Dark Brown

Patterned Paper:
Softball Images

Adhesive

Journaling Marker:
Black

Patterned-paper Photo Corners

- Cut a square from the cardstock to the desired dimensions. Keep in mind that each square will make two photo corners.

- Cut the square in half along the diagonal to form two triangles.

- Adhere each triangle in place on one of the corners of your photograph.

- Repeat the process with photo corners cut from the patterned paper. Make certain when you are cutting your squares that the images on the paper have been positioned nicely to give the best presentation.

- Layer the patterned-paper photo corners on top of the cardstock photo corners and adhere in place.

Got Dirt?

Supplies

Background Cardstock:
Kraft

Layout Cardstock:
Recycled Buckskin, Chocolate

Patterned Paper:
Muted Brown Checks

Jute: Natural

Brads: Bright Green

Colored Pencil: White

Adhesive

Journaling Marker:
Black

A Play on Advertising Phrases

- To help set the theme for your scrapbook page(s), a play on common advertising phrases is a great way to come up with a title for your scrapbook page(s). In this case, "got dirt?" for the photograph here of the little girl with the mud mustache.

- Write the phrase on a piece of cardstock and accent it with a patterned-paper mat.

FYI: This method for titling works great as page headers and/or journaling strips, blocks, and tags. Using actual phrases is also enjoyable, but keep in mind that many of these phrases are copyrighted and you may not publish your scrapbook if you use them. Some other advertising favorites include "Where's the Beef?," "The King of Country," and "Who Ya Gonna Call? Ghostbusters!"

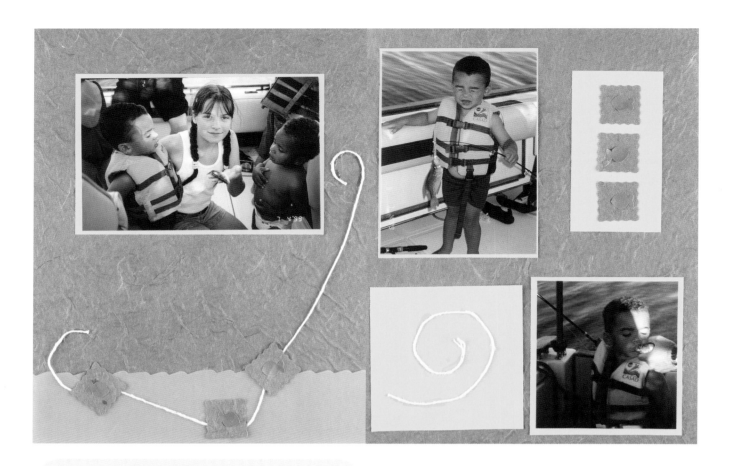

Fishy Kisses

Supplies

Background Handmade Paper: Blue

Layout Cardstock:
Metallic Gold, Yellow

Vellum: Green

String: White

Paper Punches:
Scalloped Blocks, Small Fish

Adhesive

Journaling Marker:
Black

Heavily-textured
Handmade-paper Backgrounds

- Substitute using a background cardstock with heavily textured handmade paper. It is generally sturdy enough to withstand the application of almost any embellishment.

- In addition, accent blocks can be punched from the handmade paper and used as matting for the paper-punched images. In this case, the fish have been centered on top of scalloped blocks that were punched from the handmade paper.

My Sunshine

Supplies

Background Patterned Paper:
Yellow Plaid

Layout Cardstock:
Dark Brown, White

Handmade Paper: Yellow

Stickers:
Letters & Numbers, Sunflowers,
Squiggly Border

Miniature Sunflower Bouquet

Adhesive

Journaling Marker:
Black

Patterned-paper Backgrounds

- Choose an appropriate patterned paper for the background of your scrapbook page(s).

- If the background is going to have many embellishments, it will be necessary to strengthen the background to support the embellishments. To do this, adhere the patterned paper to a sheet of cardstock. Keep in mind that some patterned papers are available in a cardstock weight.

- Continue with the design of your scrapbook page(s).

Road Trip

Supplies

Background Patterned Paper:
Road Map with Muted Center

Background Cardstock:
Yellow Parchment

Layout Cardstock: Dark Brown, Chocolate,
Moss Green, Ivory, Kraft, Orange,
Recycled White, Yellow

Preprinted Car Artwork • Memorabilia Pocket

Paper Punches: Carrot, Cloud, Coffee Cup

Precut Tags: Kraft Paper

Embroidery Floss: White • Adhesive

Journaling Markers: Assorted Colors

Repetitious Journaling

- To help set the theme for your scrapbook page(s), repetitious journaling might be a great alternative.

- Write the same sentiment several times, randomly spaced, on a piece of cardstock. In this case, the saying "are we there yet?" repeated time and again is the perfect phrase for any scrapbook page that involves children and traveling.

- Cut out the piece of cardstock and adhere it to a precut tag.

Daddy & Me

Supplies

Background Cardstock:
Blue, Lavender

Layout Cardstock:
Blue, Olive Green, Khaki, Recycled White

Vellum: Clear

Stickers: Kitchen Assortment

Miniature Brads: Black

Paper Punch: Heart

Silk Ribbon, $1/4$" Wide: Brown

Adhesive

Journaling Markers: Assorted Colors

Recipe Pages

- Make up your own recipe for love, fun, or any special occasion.

- Write each step of the recipe on a separate piece of cardstock.

- Place stickers on each of these pieces of cardstock.

- Adhere each one to the background page(s).

- Cut a piece of vellum slightly taller and slightly narrower or slightly shorter and slightly wider than each of the pieces of cardstock.

- Place the pieces of vellum over each of the pieces of cardstock and secure with one miniature brad placed at each corner.

I Love
Dinosaurs

Supplies

Background Cardstock: Recycled Cayenne, Recycled Rust
Layout Cardstock: Goldenrod, Olive Green, Kraft
Paper Punches: $1/2$" Circle, Maple Leaf, Oak Leaf, $1/2$" Square
Hole Punch: $1/4$" Diameter
Jute: Dark Green, Natural • Burlap Cord
Adhesive • Journaling Markers: Assorted Colors

Angled-section Photograph

- Cut the photograph you are using in a zigzag manner from top to bottom.

- Mat each angled section of the photograph, making certain the width of the mat is exact on all sides. In this case, a $1/8$" mat was used and is the recommended width for this technique.

- Position the matted sections of photograph on your scrapbook page(s) in the appropriate order to form the original photograph.

- Allow approximately $1/8$" of space between each section so a small portion of the background cardstock shows through. Adhere in place.

A Note from the Author . . .

I believe in the saying, "Do what you love and you will do well."
I heard Oprah say that once, and I adapt it to every aspect of
my life. I love Oprah, but who doesn't.

I first walked into a scrapbook store when my daughter, Olivia,
was a few months old. Like most people who start scrapbooking,
I took up this hobby to capture my daughter's childhood on paper.
It quickly evolved to a passion and has now taken over my small
house. But, I don't care—I love it and I think it's good for the soul.

I gather ideas from every source I can get my hands on:
pictures, friends, nature, trips, and books. I love the freedom to
express myself completely. It's a great relationship—my scrapbooks,
my supplies, and myself. I get lost in the creativity and I feel less guilty
than I would if it were chocolate—but that's another story!

More than anything, I love being able to share my love for scrapbooking with my five-year-old daughter.
She sits right next to me when I'm scrapbooking and creates in her very own way or we'll sit down and go
over the baby pictures in her books. I can't imagine a pastime more fulfilling or rewarding than this.

Metric Conversion Chart

| | | | INCHES TO MILLIMETRES AND CENTIMETRES | | | |
| | | | MM-Millimetres | CM-Centimetres | | |
INCHES	MM	CM	INCHES	CM	INCHES	CM
1/8	3	0.9	9	22.9	30	76.2
1/4	6	0.6	10	25.4	31	78.7
3/8	10	1.0	11	27.9	32	81.3
1/2	13	1.3	12	30.5	33	83.8
5/8	16	1.6	13	33.0	34	86.4
3/4	19	1.9	14	35.6	35	88.9
7/8	22	2.2	15	38.1	36	91.4
1	25	2.5	16	40.6	37	94.0
1 1/4	32	3.2	17	43.2	38	96.5
1 1/2	38	3.8	18	45.7	39	99.1
1 3/4	44	4.4	19	48.3	40	101.6
2	51	5.1	20	50.8	41	104.1
2 1/2	64	6.4	21	53.3	42	106.7
3	76	7.6	22	55.9	43	109.2
3 1/2	89	8.9	23	58.4	44	111.8
4	102	10.2	24	61.0	45	114.3
4 1/2	114	11.4	25	63.5	46	116.8
5	127	12.7	26	66.0	47	119.4
6	152	15.2	27	68.6	48	121.9
7	178	17.8	28	71.1	49	124.5
8	203	20.3	29	73.7	50	127.0

Index

A Day at the Farm 94–95
A Note from the Author 126
A Play on Advertising Phrases 119
A Special Boy 27
A Special Girl 10
A Summer Day 17
Adding Dimension with Foam Dots 58
Adding Drama with
   Black Cardstock 82
Ahoy Matey 33
All Boy 96
All Four Seasons 78–79
Amusement Park Fun 105
Angels in the Garden 42–43
Angled-section
   Photograph 124–125
Arches National Park 102
Autumn Harvest 114
Baby Love 67
Beach Bums 38
Bead Dangle Embellishment 39
Boy Wonder 36–37
Boys 48
Bring on the Sun 53
Buggy for Bugs 52
Bunny Ears 57

Cardstock Photo Corners 87
Cardstock Ribbon 114
Chalking 57
Chapter 1: Making Memories 10–39
Chapter 2:
   Sharing Special Times 40–63
Chapter 3: Family Fun 64–85
Chapter 4: Candid Moments 86–125
Charm Embellishment 28
Checkerboard Backgrounds 80
Christmas Time Favorites 62–63
Clothesline with Miniature
   Clothespins 78–79
Color Tinting Black-and-White
   Photographs 111
Combining Geometric Shapes 53
Concealing the Corner of a
   Photograph 71
Considering Proportions 47
Country Girls 80
Cousins Make the
   Best Friends 54–55
Cowboy Kids 45
Craft Wire Embellishment 17
Curling Craft Wire 69
Daddy & Me 123

Die-cut & Metal-rimmed Tags 22–23
Die-cut Tag Tea Bags 65
Dimensional Photo Mats 72–73
Displaying Special Schoolwork 46
Distressed & Aged Cardstock 45
Don't Forget How Special
   You Are 50–51
Easter Favorites 22–23
Embellishing with Miniatures 87
Everything Tastes Better
   at Grandma's 26
Eyelets In a
   Decorative Capacity 25
Eyelets In a
   Functional Capacity 24
Fall Leaves 34–35
Falling in Love with the Ocean 28
Family Sledding Day 30–31
Family Ties 20–21
Father, Brother, Son & Friend 99
Faux-stitching Accents 47
Fiber & Bead Tassel
   Tag Embellishment 112–113
Filmstrip Photo Placement 106–107
Fishy Kisses 120
Five Generations of Strong Women 64

Formal Family Photos 14–15
General Information 8
Ghosts, Witches & Creepy Spiders ... 90
Girl Power 25
Glass Bead Embellishment 28
Glitter Embellishment 76
Glued-bead Embellishment 48
Glued-button Embellishment 27
Gone Fishin' 89
Got Dirt? 119
Grandma's Men 115
Grandma's Sweater 56
Halloween 77
Hand-cut Tags 20–21
Hand-folded Envelope
   for Silk Roses 41
Handmade-paper Art 42–43
Hand-sewn Embellishment 34–35
Hanging Ladder Signs 67
Hanging Looped-wire
   Embellishment 44
Hanging Signs 32
Hanging Vines 97
Happy Campers 72–73
Heart Dangle Embellishment 84–85
Heavily-textured Handmade-paper
   Backgrounds 120
Heirloom Embellishment 58
Helping Hands 11
Here Comes Trouble 117
High School Graduation 70
Hole-punched Cardstock Lace 41
Huntin' Wabbits 32
Hush Little Baby 75
I Love Chocolate 83
I Love Dinosaurs 124–125
I Love Mom the Most 108–109
I Love Snowmen 46
It's a Grandma Thing 58
It's a Grandpa Thing 59
Jute-strung Alphabet Letters 99
Lace Contouring 116
Lacing Eyelets 27
Laser-cut Die-cut Embellishment 80
Layered Paper-punch Embellishment 10
Layered Photo Mats 16
Layered Torn-paper Page Borders &
   Torn-paper Photo Mats 12
Layered Vellum Strips 115
Letter Sticker Tiles 33
Little League Softball 118
Live, Laugh, Love 49
Matching Patterned Papers to
   Wardrobe Fabrics 14–15
Matted-brad Embellishment 100–101
Matted Panel of Buttons 54–55
Matting Pewter Word Blocks 50–51
Memorabilia Pocket Embellishment 28
Mesh Embellishment 32
Metal-rimmed Vellum Tags 66
Metric Conversion Chart 126
Microbead Embellishment 40
Miniature Brad Embellishment 18–19

Mixing Black-and-White &
   Color Photographs 18–19
Mom's Childhood 116
Mother's Day 16
Multicolored-bead Embellishment 86
Multicolored Photo Mats 30–31
My Favorite Aunt 74
My Sunshine 121
My Valentine 66
Number Sequencing
   on Photographs 86
Our First Haircut Together 103
Our Little Helper 87
Paper-punched Letter Tiles 13
Paper-punched Windows 108–109
Paper-ribbon Art 62–63
Paper-ribbon Flowers 91
Patchwork & Embellished
   Hand-cut Tag 59
Patchwork Page Borders 114
Patterned-paper Backgrounds 121
Patterned-paper Photo Corners 118
Pewter Letter-block Embellishment 49
Pewter Word-block Embellishment ... 50–51
Photo Overlays 33
Photo Overlay Tic-Tac-Toe Board 83
Photo Toppers 116
Placing Photographs on an Angle 70
Playground Fun 104
Precut Kraft-paper Tags 49
Precious One 40
Preface 8
Preschool Graduation 71
Pretty as a Poppy 91
Primary-colored Checkerboard
   Background 104
Pumpkin Patch 18–19
Puppy Love 60–61
Raised Photo Accent 117
Recipe Pages 123
Red Rock Ruins 12
Repetitious Journaling 122
Repetitious Journaling Blocks 75
Rhinestone Embellishment 29
River Bridge Picnic 92
Road Trip 122
Roses Are Red 82
Rumble Young Man 47
Rustic Shape Embellishment 48
Santa 100–101
Senior Prom 83
Sentiment Phrasing 50–51
Sewn-button Embellishment 54–55
Shaker Window Embellishment 81
Silk-ribbon Embellishment 16
Silly Friends 29
Single Photo-corner Accent 26
Sisters 68
Sisters & Friends 69
Sisters by Chance Friends by Choice 44
Skipping Stones 13
Snowman Stareoff 98
Special Little Angel 84–85

Spook Party 76
Stay Curious 81
Stenciled-letter Tiles 92
Stenciling Page Borders 77
Sticker Tiles 52
Stop & Smell the Roses 41
String Art 26
String Whiskers & Hair 90
Sugar & Spice 39
Sunflower Sweetheart 111
Tea-dyed Handmade Paper 38
Tea for Two 65
Thank Heaven for Little Girls 24
There's No Place Like Home 110
Threaded-bead Embellishment 39
Threaded Leather-cord
   Embellishment 96
Threaded-ribbon Embellishment 56
3-D Journaling Tags
   Using Raffia 94–95
3-D Journaling Tags
   Using Thick Yarn 98
Torn Handmade Paper 36–37
Torn-paper Art 29
Torn-paper Horizons 60–61
Torn-paper Page Borders 11
Torn Tags 34–35
Torn-vellum Art 112–113
Transforming Paper-punch Images 88
Tweet-Hearts 97
Twig Fishing Pole 89
Two-toned Horizontal
   Backgrounds 10
Two-toned Letters 105
Using a Single Photograph 75
Using Card-making Miniatures 93
Using Enlarged Photographs 102
Using Paper Clips for
   Attaching Embellishments 103
Using Paper-punched Images
   for Letters 104
Using School Colors on
   Page Layouts 70
Vellum-matted Mesh 66
Vellum Pocket 68
Vellum Windows 64
Vellum-wrapped &
   Stitched Cardstock 29
Vertical Journaling Strips 74
Vertical Strips with Vellum Overlays 38
Visions of Sugarplums 88
Who Says I Can't Have
   My Cake & Eat It Too? 86
Wire-strung Punched Images 71
Wire-wrapped Wooden Shapes 69
Word Tiles 52
Wound Embroidery Floss
   Embellishment 36–37
Wound-string Embellishment 30–31
Wound-yarn Embellishment 56
Yarn-fiber Writing 110
Yellowstone National Park 112–113
You're a Natural 106–107